FOOTPRINTS ON MALEKULA

Bernard Deacon on Malekula, 1927.

Footprints on Malekula

a memoir of Bernard Deacon
by MARGARET GARDINER

with a Preface by
RODNEY NEEDHAM
and an Introduction by
PETER GATHERCOLE

'an association in which the free development of each
is the condition for the free development of all'

Free Association Books / London / 1987

Published September 1987 by
Free Association Books
26 Freegrove Road
London N7 9RQ

Originally published by
The Salamander Press Edinburgh Ltd

British Library Cataloguing in Publication Data
Gardiner, Margaret
    Footprints on Malekula.
    1. Deacon, Bernard   2. Ethnologists—
    Great Britain—Biography
    I. Title
    306'.092'4   GN21.D4

ISBN   0 946960 97 6 hbk
        0 946960 98 4 pbk

Designed by Tom Fenton
Printed and bound in Great Britain by
Latimer Trend & Company Ltd, Plymouth

Acknowledgments

All the photographs of Bernard Deacon were given to me by his mother: the photograph of Amanrantus, who was guide and interpreter to Bernard on many expeditions, was given to me by his two sons, Aïleh and Aïar Rantes who described their father to me as 'Mr Deacon's friend'. The photographs of my visit to Malekula were taken by Kirk Huffman, who gave them to me for this book and to whom I am also most grateful for both arranging the visit and accompanying me there.

Among those who have encouraged me to write and to publish this memoir I would specially like to thank James Fenton, Tom Fenton, Peter Gathercole, the late Professor Myer Fortes, Esther Salaman, and my son, Martin Bernal.

List of Illustrations

Contents

Preface

Bernard Deacon, a talented Cambridge anthropologist, died in 1927, in the New Hebrides, at the age of twenty-four. His professional renown was to be made by a report he had written on the 'six-class' marriage system of Ambrym. This form of social organisation made a remarkable theoretical stir, and it has since remained an important topic of debate and reanalysis.

Deacon left also an unpublished and highly personal record of his expedition, in letters to Margaret Gardiner which she has reproduced in this poignant memoir. They convey, if obliquely, something of the great impact made by an exotic civilisation on an intensely introspective young ethnographer, subjected to bewildering impulses of sentiment and scientific commitment. A striking aspect of these letters is indeed that they are preponderantly about Deacon himself: the people among whom he lived are very much in the background. This is not a failure in concern, for Deacon's writings testify to his close attention to his subjects and to his sympathy for them. What the focus of the letters reveals is a neglected but crucial component in field research: namely how the extremities of the experience can force the ethnographer to come to terms with himself. The manner in which Deacon wrote to Margaret Gardiner is a unique evidence of this moral ordeal and an invaluable clue to the character of a lost brilliance.

The other side of the matter is that the letters illumine by reflection the person to whom they were addressed, and the tribulations that she too had to endure. Margaret Gardiner writes on her own account to fine effect, and an impressive part of her moving composition is the ethnographic capacity that she herself deploys in recounting her visit to Deacon's grave in Vanuatu. No one else could have written this memoir of a dual tragedy, and she has done so with an admirable blend of reticence and disclosure.

RODNEY NEEDHAM

All Souls College, Oxford
December 1983

[ix]

Introduction

When Margaret Gardiner showed me her memoir of Bernard Deacon, I suggested that it would be useful if a brief account could be added on the significance of his anthropological work. Margaret agreed, and persuaded me to write it. Her memoir, of course, speaks for itself. This introduction gives only the setting of Deacon's fieldwork.

The island of Malekula, where Deacon worked in 1926–7, is part of the new Pacific republic of Vanuatu, which was established in 1980. Before then it had been the Anglo-French Condominium of the New Hebrides, set up in 1906 in the interests of these two powers. The archipelago was once described by Douglas L. Oliver, as, because of its colonial history, 'one of the unhealthiest, wildest, most mistreated, and most mismanaged spots on earth'. It never attracted a large number of colonists. But from the 1840s traders began to arrive, and they were followed by recruiters seeking labour to work the sugar plantations, mainly in Queensland. By the 1880s about 20,000 men had been recruited, often forcibly, for this work. Planters began to introduce a range of cash crops, which radically altered the economy. Christian missions of various denominations competed for converts and introduced a measure of literacy. Under these pressures traditional cultures changed, sometimes very rapidly. Labour was recruited for cash-cropping which changed patterns of settlement, and there was increasing demand for imported goods, notably liquor and guns. The islanders suffered severely from the social and psychological effects of colonial rule, and from introduced diseases: measles, influenza, tuberculosis, smallpox, whooping cough, scarlet fever, meningitis and diphtheria. It has been estimated that between 1892 and 1935 the population declined from just under 100,000 to 45,000.

When Deacon arrived in Malekula in January 1926, anthropological interest in the area – stimulated in part by the decline of traditional cultures – had existed for about forty years. But there had been very few detailed studies based on prolonged fieldwork. The stimulus for research came primarily from Cambridge University, where A. C. Haddon, the founder of anthropological teaching, in effect created a centre for Pacific Islands' research. He led a famous pioneer expedition to the Torres Straits in 1898, where one of his colleagues, W. H. R. Rivers, instituted the study of kinship as central to the examination of social organisation. Rivers made a brief visit to some of the New Hebrides' islands in 1908, mainly to obtain information on kinship, but it was John Layard, a pupil of Rivers, who made the first detailed study. He worked for over a year in 1914–15 on the Small Islands off north-east Malekula. After the Great War C. B. Humphreys went to the southern New Hebrides and T. T. Barnard to islands in the centre of the group. Rivers died suddenly in the summer of 1922, many of his research problems unsolved.

Layard's field material was superb, but he was unable to write it up because his health had become seriously affected, a situation only partly remedied when his book, *Stone Men of Malekula*, was eventually published in 1942. He was able to give Deacon considerable advice, but at that time most of Malekula remained an unknown ethnographic map.

Deacon therefore faced a most difficult task in attempting to record and understand the significance of Malekulan ethnography. He had to rely on his day-to-day experience, linguistic ability and perceptive insight. This would have been a gruelling responsibility for any older and more experienced fieldworker. Deacon had received only one year's training at Cambridge, and had no field experience at all. The amount and quality of his field notes demonstrate his brilliance as an anthropologist, and Margaret Gardiner's memoir amplifies this in a most moving way. His letters illuminate his periods of intellectual discovery, his capacity for work, and his times of exhaustion, loneliness and uncertainty. One reads them with admiration. Tragically, Bernard Deacon died of blackwater fever on March 12th, 1927, a few weeks after his twenty-fourth birthday, as he was about to leave Malekula, his fieldwork completed. He had been appointed to a Lectureship in Social Anthropology at the University of Sydney, under Professor A. Radcliffe-Brown, where he intended to write up his material.

What was life on Malekula like? Typically, a Malekulan man

spent much of it buying his way through a sequence of graded societies which were centred on his club house. (In some areas Deacon listed up to thirty-two grades open for an individual's advancement, though not all were taken up in each case.) In a sense, however, the graded societies, and the activities centred on them, were only a prelude to the hereafter, for a man consecrated himself as he advanced in grade to *ensure* his successful after-life. In southern Malekula the after-life of a man of appropriate status was commemorated by the manufacture of his effigy (*rambaramp*), an example of which was bought by Deacon and is now in the University Museum of Archaeology and Anthropology at Cambridge. All rituals connected with the graded societies were marked by the ceremonial sacrifice of tusked pigs, the erection of stone monuments and wooden gongs to the memory of ancestors, and the production of sculpture and other pieces of art which were often highly dramatic and sophisticated productions in their own right.

Within this status society, pigs were the major form of determining wealth, especially animals with deformed lower tusks, the upper ones being knocked out to facilitate their growth. Pigs were important for sacrifice in connection with graded society rituals, but they were also required as payment for special services by sorcerers or craftsmen, and for other ceremonial exchanges. If pigs were borrowed, the debt had to be repaid by others having the same tusk length as the loaned animals would have had at the time of repayment. Malekula, therefore, was composed, not of 'primitive' societies, but of very complex social groups retaining many elements of their traditional life. The recent dramatic resurgence of 'custom' throughout Vanuatu is due partly to the existence of detailed records such as those compiled by Deacon, which have helped to educate the people concerning what they have lost or nearly lost.

Apart from a number of papers, the major results of Deacon's work were published under his name in the book *Malekula: a Vanishing People in the New Hebrides*, edited by Camilla H. Wedgwood, with a preface by Haddon. It is rich in ethnography, contains many personal insights, and remains an essential study for any appreciation of the anthropology and recent history of Vanuatu.

Deacon quickly found that Malekulan cultures were extremely

varied (today there are at least a hundred living languages through-out Vanuatu), and that it was impossible to replicate the range of his enquiries into each aspect of life as he moved into a new area. Thus *Malekula* is inevitably an uneven book. What is remarkable, however, is the amount and quality of detail it contains, particularly concerning ceremonial and other esoteric aspects of island life. This has proved to be invaluable to later workers.

Extensive anthropological work of a similar kind was undertaken on Malekula by the Frenchman, Jean Guiart, in the early 1950s. He has written of Deacon's research in these terms: 'It was very moving for me to realise that, after such a long time, it was possible to verify Deacon's data, and, on the more important points, to get identical information, sometimes with a few more details. As I went through South West Bay, I found that his tomb was still only earth-covered and I had a modest cement monument erected with the necessary explanations engraved thereon.'

Deacon's most important discovery, however, was at a theoretical level. This was due, somewhat ironically, to work done not on Malekula but on the nearby island of Ambrym, where he went for six weeks early in 1927. There, he wrote to Haddon, he found 'a system of marriage classes, still in full working, of the type of those among the Central Australian tribes, though not exactly corres-ponding with any Australian system . . . For me it clears up a great deal, even in Malekula. It bears, I think, on the general question of anomalous marriages, dual organisation, and Melanesian history. I have tried to sketch out in the notes to Brown how it clears up problems, modifies Rivers' work, and so on. To me it is like a sudden illumination.' This discovery of a six-class marriage system was indeed a major achievement. It made sense of data collected by Rivers in 1914, and worked on by others subsequently. Barnard had suggested in his Ph.D. thesis submitted in the previous year that such a system existed, and Deacon may have read at least a draft of the thesis before he left Cambridge. But now he had demonstrated the actuality of the system.

In his book, *The Building of British Social Anthropology*, where these matters are discussed, Ian Langham has argued that Deacon's discovery was a test case whereby British social anthropology validated itself as an academic discipline. Certainly it received major attention in the literature. Details were first published in the

Journal of the Anthropological Institute alongside papers by Radcliffe-Brown and Brenda Seligman emphasising the importance of the discovery. But the final comment on Bernard Deacon's work should be Layard's:

> Deacon had read through most of my field notes before going to Malekula, and it was on my recommendation that he went to South West Bay. His work on this and other parts of Malekula, published posthumously by Miss Camilla Wedgwood, is a model of scientific observation of an unusually interesting kind, and his discovery of a six-section system of kinship on the neighbouring island of Ambrim was a landmark in the history of anthropology and has, as such, been used as the basis for the discussion of kinship in this volume. I wish to take this opportunity of expressing the great admiration I feel for him not only as a scientific investigator but also as a man, and at the same time thank his editor for her great service in undertaking the difficult task of preparing his field notes for publication.

Time has emphasised the correctness of this judgment.

PETER GATHERCOLE

References

Deacon, A. B., 'The Regulation of Marriage in Ambrym', *Journal of the Anthropological Institute*, 57: 325–42, 1927.
Deacon, A. B., *Malekula: a Vanishing People of the New Hebrides*, London, Routledge, 1934.
Guiart, Jean, 'Native Society in the New Hebrides: the Big Nambas of Northern Malekula', *Mankind*, 4: 439–46, 1953.
Langham, Ian, *The Building of British Social Anthropology: W. H. R. Rivers and his Cambridge Disciples in the Development of Kinship Studies, 1898–1931*, Dordrecht, Reidel, 1981.
Layard, John, *Stone Men of Malekula*, London, Chatto and Windus, 1942.
Oliver, Douglas L., *The Pacific Islands*, Cambridge, Harvard University Press, 1951.

I would like to thank Dr Michael Allen, of the University of Sydney, for assistance, especially concerning his own research in Vanuatu.

Author's Note

In my opening paragraph I refer to *Malekula: a Vanishing People in the New Hebrides* by A. Bernard Deacon, edited by Camilla H. Wedgwood with a preface by A. C. Haddon. When I was writing this memoir I was not aware of the extent of the recognition still given by anthropologists to Bernard's work. That the book was not the one that Bernard himself would have written was well understood by its editor, Camilla Wedgwood. In May 1928 she wrote to her colleague, W. E. Armstrong, whose lectures Bernard had attended and with whom he had had a warm friendship, 'I am gradually breaking the back of the job of getting Deacon's notes into order, & discovering how much material there is . . . My room is at present littered with genealogies & tables of comparative terms . . . But of course the bulk of the material is on Secret Societies. There are about seven in one district alone & the distribution of these in other parts of the island with their various grade-names, associations with fertility, death, mythology, prehistoric pottery, incision etc. etc. is turning my hair grey . . . I suppose I shall eventually reduce it to an intelligible form, but at present I feel rather like Alice in Wonderland.'

In March the following year she wrote – once more to W. E. Armstrong – 'I shall be glad when it is all finished. It is a depressing occupation for again and again, when I thought I was on the track of something exciting the trail has failed – an unfinished sentence or a medley of native technical terms. Occasionally the culture comes alive but I am afraid the deadness of the book will reflect only too faithfully the moribund condition of the people.'

It did indeed seem at that time that the Malekulans were a vanishing people, that disease and despair would soon finally wipe them out. They had lost heart, they had become cynical. 'Sons and daughters seem to belong to a culture totally different from that of their parents,' Bernard wrote to me. 'To some extent they keep on doing the same things, but from inertia or boredom, not from any inner necessity. There is an absence of direction.'

They didn't vanish: Bernard was there at the nadir when a disastrous series of epidemics had made the future of the island populations appear hopeless. But improved medicines and the medical care brought by the missionaries, together with the ending of tribal warfare, halted the decline: the population increased once more and the will to live was restored.

M.G.

Letters are more than recollections, the very lifeblood of the past is stored up in them; they are *the past, exactly as it was, preserved from destruction and decay.*

ALEXANDER HERZEN

Footprints on Malekula

After my death there will, I think, be no one left who remembers Bernard Deacon: his only memorial perhaps the massive book stitched together with patient scholarship from the notes he made during his fourteen months' ethnological fieldwork on the island of Malekula in the New Hebrides. But it isn't the book that Bernard would have written.

> Whatever work I am doing now has got to such a hopeless state of interdependence [he wrote to me from Malekula] that I find it terribly difficult to get it down on paper. The consciousness of a connexion between 2 things forms gradually, till it becomes a general hypothesis for the working out of a number of problems: these lead on again, the thing becomes unconsciously modified, and you find everything needs rearranging. Your sets of facts remain constant, but the nature of their relation to one another is changed by every fresh fact: it is fearfully necessary to go through notes & *put in the altered relations*, or otherwise the notes may be quite misleading and almost without value if you died suddenly before 'writing up'. And generally you are unconscious that you have been associating things in a certain way till it becomes suddenly necessary to associate them in another. I'm sorry to be so trite, but it is really rather interesting how almost impossible it is to bring a thing into a region of thought without setting up a whole lot of irrelevant associations to other things in that field. It's ghastly how conventional one is, in thought – I mean, the deepest, most analytic or most imaginative thought: the conventions linked with emotions are far less terrible, you can make allowances for them and let them bide, I suppose, without much harm.

But Bernard did die suddenly before 'writing up' and so the book must remain, inevitably, only an approximation.

In his preface to the book, Dr A. C. Haddon, who had just

retired as Reader in Ethnology in Cambridge, detailed Bernard's astonishing academic record – the many scholarships and prizes, and the three first-class honours degrees in Natural Sciences, Mediaeval and Modern Languages, and Anthropology. Haddon also quoted the opinion of Bernard's headmaster at Nottingham High School that Bernard had been the ablest pupil that he had ever had, and that of the vicar of the village in which Bernard's mother lived, who had written that for sheer brilliance he had never met Bernard's equal. And a fellow student had written, 'My general feeling about him is that he was even more important as a human being than as an ethnologist. He was not, I think, an easy person to know well, for although he talked brilliantly about many things he scarcely ever talked about himself. . . He also seemed to me utterly lacking in conceit, as though it did not matter to him at all that he had an infinitely better intellect than anyone else in the room.'

Of all this brilliance and achievement I knew nothing when I first met Bernard, and nothing either of his background. I only gradually discovered that he had been born in January 1903 in Nicolaev in South Russia where his father, a man of outstanding intelligence, had worked for a shipping firm. Both his parents were village folk who came from the same village in Nottinghamshire, and his mother, I think, had at one time worked in a neighbouring big house. When he was thirteen Bernard was sent back to England to go to Nottingham High School and to live with an uncle, a clergyman of very strict and narrow views. He was intensely unhappy, cut off from his parents and from Russia, which he had so loved. His father's firm collapsed in the turmoil of the early days of the revolution and his mother, deeply distressed by the death of her baby daughter and the total disruption of their lives, had a breakdown from which it took her many years to recover. Finally she arrived back in England and settled in a cottage in the village of Blyth, near Worksop, while her husband became a British consul in Rumania – I think it was in Galatz – where he remained until he retired and joined his wife in Blyth.

Russia always held Bernard's imagination: it was where he felt his roots to be. 'Margou' he wrote to me – he often called me by the pet name my family sometimes used –

Margou, we must go to Russia sometime, and to South Russia. Something in me that is living and young and direct, and yet age-old somehow, belongs there. Perhaps it's all pathology. I don't know. I do feel terribly a life, a capacity for unbounded sacrifice and creation there, which I don't feel in the West. No, perhaps it's just imagination: but so real then that it scarcely matters. I never knew Russia properly, only as a child and a boy. I remember families and events and the changes of the year, summer in the *datchas*, visits of the Emperor, cossacks, the conservatoire, the clang and boom of bells, Easter, soldiers at their prayers – how fatally beautiful it all seems, how deep and moving and more than beautiful. Was it just *l'ancien régime*? Summer on the steppes, endless, endless summer, stirring me to madness that I could not yield myself to it utterly, going further and further into the illimitable steppe! There is a power in it I have never found in England: I loathed the England I first knew, I was sick of it – the Midlands.

Bernard also wrote to me, in a letter from Malekula, about his life in the Midlands. He had been reading a copy of *The Rainbow*, borrowed from a planter, the only man on the island who had a library:

. . . lovely stuff. I think one with *Sons and Lovers* & *The White Peacock*. The Mexican I think a failure. It is strange in *The Rainbow* reading about Ilkeston & Nottingham: I spent nearly five years of my life there, most of my adolescence with all the concomitant *Sturm und Drang*, brooding and mysticism and queer, unsure 'first love' – great periods when everything was distorted & intensified and values of experience shifted about irresponsibly and rapidly. And strange how out of injury and foulness would come clear diamond, catching and cupping and burning with the full noon of another world. The universe seemed much more coordinated then, than ever since: there seemed to be some relation between different fields of experience which gave ultimately a unity which I remember but I don't feel it now. I could not doubt the thing when it was happening, I cannot but doubt it now that it's unrealizable. I was working for my scholarsip at Trinity at the time of what Lawrence has called 'an ecstasy of bitterness' – or 'the bitterness of ecstasy' – I'm sorry – in an atmosphere, now I recollect it, very like his – Ursula's – But when I got through I was so horribly thankful that I resolved never to run exams and crises together again. Which I didn't. It was mercenary?

I first met Bernard at a tea party in Trinity College, Cambridge in the spring of 1925, when I was in my second year at Newnham. I noticed the tall young man, dark-haired and dark-eyed, with an olive complexion, standing quietly at the side of the room. A bit of a dandy, I thought, with his double-breasted jacket and walking stick. He had a slightly foreign look and there seemed to be something mysterious about him. A secret kind of person, I decided, and I knew at once that I very much wanted to meet him. So I went up to him and asked him his name and which was his college – it was Trinity – and what was he reading? Anthropology.

After a while 'You ought to come and have tea with me some day,' he said, and told me the address of his digs.

I waited eagerly for the invitation but it didn't come. Then, one afternoon, a little breathless, I walked into his room. He was sitting at the table, writing, with his back to me, and he looked round, startled.

'I was working,' he said, as though it needed some apology. He closed his books. 'I'll see about getting us some tea.'

It was nearing exam time, but I wasn't taking work very seriously. For me there was too much else in Cambridge, all the intoxicating excitements of meeting people, of talk, of ideas. And besides, I didn't really need to work. But Bernard did. As well as being intensely interested in his subject he was, for all his elegant appearance and relaxed manner, extremely poor and entirely dependent upon scholarships and grants. This was his last year in Cambridge: his idea had been to try for the consular service but since he was too young to sit the exam, he'd had to decide what to read as an extra during his final year. He had chosen anthropology: it was almost a haphazard choice, a stop-gap, a mere diploma. But Dr Haddon had persuaded him to read for the tripos.

Bernard's brilliance soon became apparent to the Faculty of Archaeology and Anthropology, and when he produced a remark-able paper on 'The Kakihan Society of Ceram and New Guinea Initiation Cults' – which was subsequently published in *Folk-Lore* – Dr Haddon suggested that he should drop his consular plans

[4]

in order to make an extensive study of the ethnography of Malekula, an island where a certain amount of fieldwork had already been done, but little had so far been published. Bernard agreed, and in order to make it possible he was awarded a studentship and a grant and a considerable extension of his Trinity scholarship.

We began to meet quite often and our friendship grew, but in what, at that time, seemed to me an unusual way. I took it for granted then that every young man I got to know would fall in love with me: it seemed inevitable, part of the natural order of things. But Bernard was different: I knew he liked me, I thought he liked me very much but there was also always a certain aloofness, and he very rarely spoke about himself. He did, however, tell me that he knew a girl in Cambridge called Vera – a 'town' girl, not a university girl – who was very beautiful.

'Are you in love with her?' I asked.

He considered. 'No, I don't think so. I just want to take off her clothes and make her lie on blue cushions, like the Maya.'

This perturbed and puzzled me, as it did also when he told me that while in Paris with a friend they had visited a brothel.

'It wasn't very interesting,' he said.

These glimpses of Bernard frightened me: they seemed so utterly foreign, so matter of fact and alien and so far away from any relationship we had. He was still for me mysterious, a kind of secret person. Not that he was hiding anything: he was open, frank and completely truthful and yet, at the same time, reticent. It was only slowly that I came to realise he had depths of experience and perception I could never reach and that some rare alchemy had given a richness of life to his thinking and feeling beyond anything that it was in me to experience.

I don't remember many details of that Cambridge time, only a miniature scene here and there. I remember Bernard talking to me about mineralogy, one of the subjects he had read in his first tripos.

'But isn't it rather dull?' I asked. 'Rather a dead-end subject? Just listing all those stones and inanimate things?'

'You're completely wrong,' he said. 'It's not like that at all. It's fascinating.' And so, when he spoke about it, it was.

And I remember how once he mentioned his mother, and he

suddenly stood still and looked at me with a smile of tenderness and amusement at the thought of her.

'My mother,' he said. 'You ought to meet her. She fusses tremendously around the house. I tell her to stop: it's ridiculous, I say. You're only moving the dust from one place to another. But of course she takes no notice of me.'

I remember, too, running into Bernard in King's Parade on the day when some of the tripos results had been posted up outside the Senate. After asking me how I had done, he told me that he had again got a first. It had been a certainty that he would get one, but he seemed unusually happy, a little relieved, a little elated.

In the summer holidays my parents always rented a country house where they gave a series of house parties to which my brothers and I were urged to invite our friends. I looked upon those parties as a duty rather than a pleasure, and would stay for as short a time as I decently could. But in that summer of 1925 I had invited Bernard to stay at the house they had taken in Dorset and I awaited his coming with excitement and some trepidation. I was very much in love with him.

I don't remember who else was staying there that week, apart from my two brothers, Rolf and John. The only thing I cared about was being with Bernard; no one else really existed for me. My mother, who in general disliked most of my friends, considering them to be odd and ill-mannered, liked Bernard very much.

'He's so *aristocratic*,' she said to me. In fact, he was the only one of my friends at that time who came from a working-class background.

We joined in all the prescribed rituals of those parties, the curious mixture of formality and informality that always characterised my parents' households. We went on picnics, we played charades and guessing games and pencil and paper games, we listened to the jokes about my mother's inventive malapropisms – 'mummyisms' my father used to call them – and to stories about Doswell, my parents' eccentric housemaid. And we joined in the country dancing on the lawn, organised by my brother Rolf, and we ate the long, long meals and we sang the rounds and catches that so delighted my mother.

Rose, Rose, Rose, Rose
Shall I ever see thee red?
Aye, marry, that thou shalt
If thou but stay.

Only, Bernard wasn't going to stay: he was to start for Malekula in a few weeks.

On the last day of his visit Bernard and I went for a walk. I don't remember where we went, only that we walked on and on as though we were never going to stop. He had taught me the Russian alphabet and a Russian jingle:

Чижик Пыжик, где ты был?

На Фонтанке водку пил.

Выпил рюмку, выпил две,

Зашумело в голове.

[Siskin, piskin, where have you been?
I've been to the tavern drinking vodka;
I drank one glass, I drank two,
There's a buzzing in my head.]

We chanted it together as we walked. I told him about my first meeting with Peter Mrosovsky, a friend of mine who was also a friend of Bernard's. It had been when I was fifteen years old and at school at Bedales. I was walking along the country road that bounded the school when I saw Peter, an old boy who was on a visit, strolling ahead of me. He was a Russian and very tall and very good-looking. I started to run after him; he turned, saw me and fled. But I caught him up.

'Did you want to talk to *me*?' he asked, at bay.

'Yes,' I panted. 'I want you to tell me about the Russian revolution, please.'

The Russian revolution, about which we knew so little and that little so confused, seemed to me then the most exciting thing in the world. Peter laughed. 'I think you'd better read Kropotkin,' he said. So I read Kropotkin and became, for the time being, a convinced anarchist and a great believer in three acres and a cow.

When I told Bernard this, he also laughed.

'Little rebel,' he said, mocking.

[7]

It was evening and then night, and the stars came out. Bernard showed me Algol, and told me the names of some of the constellations that I didn't know and explained about the spiral nebulae. I was cold in my cotton frock and I put my hand in the pocket of his jacket. But he didn't take it in his. He asked 'Are you cold?' and then took off his jacket and draped it round my shoulders. And so I walked back, wrapped in his warmth.

It was nearly midnight when we reached the house. I paused in the hall to glance at some portraits of Africans with the tribal slashes on their faces.

'How horrid,' I said, 'how horrid to be so mutilated.'

'Do you think so?' asked Bernard. 'I rather like it. I think it looks rather nice.'

To my annoyance, we found that my mother had been sitting up, sleepily waiting for our return.

'I thought you might be hungry,' she said, as though realising that she needed some excuse. 'There's a plate of sandwiches and I could get you some hot milk.'

Bernard left next morning and I felt utterly disconsolate: nothing had been resolved between us. He wrote to me from Trinity:

Dear Margaret

What am I to say to you? It is morning here and very fine. Lady P has been while I was away & returned me *Contraception* [a book Bernard had lent her son]. I feel very annoyed with Billy, he is unnecessarily thoughtless.

I went to Kew yesterday morning to look for a Sicca – there were Chinese cypresses, beautiful things, hibiscus bushes, tiger lilies, water plants with frosted velvet leaves like cracked wax, so dry that great drops of water shook across them without bursting, shaggy untidy trees with a sort of hair hanging from their bark, pendulous fruits dangling like fat penises of bulls – but no Siccas, so I came away. Then (no, the night before) I went to see the beggars in the crypt of St Martins, and from there along the embankment 'home', about 1.30. Vera was in London & I stayed there. She wants me to go into the country before leaving for M but it's impossible. I feel very keenly what Edith Sitwell says somewhere that the world is a thin matchboard flooring spread over a shallow hell, that all vastness has gone. Vera still feels the passage of things as momentous and irrevocable, to her all things – and especially 'love' – must move swiftly and unswervingly to their appointed end – the satirist and cynic alone stand incomprehensibly outside. Someone has done a very good & rather unpleasant study of the kind of thing – Viola Meynell? – in *Modern Lovers* I think. I'm sorry, Margaret, all this is rather unpleasant and unnecessary. I am simply feeling rather acutely how easy it is to be unfair when a relation is so asymmetrical & wish I could dissolve things which imagination alone has called into being. I suppose it is the essence of romanticism to believe that the relations of people to things in the outer world are subservient to the one relation of man to man in the inner – and I am always overwhelmed by the truth of the converse proposition . . .

Warmth and stability – what strange things to desire – no, not *à propos* of the above, but just so . . .

I'm afraid this letter is degenerating into maundering (?) about people in general.

I sat thinking in the train last night of all the 'mummyisms', and of Dozzwole, who for some reason is vivid, perhaps because I heard her and of her without seeing or talking to her. I was going to write to your mother, just so, but it seemed easier to think, writing is laborious & prosaic – a significant verbal proposition! However, I shall do so . . .

This letter seems to be full of horrid things – contraception, bulls, Vera, C., S. I should have guided it better – innate awkwardness. I suddenly feel appallingly conscious of your criticism – you and Rolf strolling in the moonlight, with a brown dress and blue earrings, Rolf disarmingly vulgar. I like it very much but it is far above me. I can only try and find a spiral nebula, something complicated . . . Rose, Rose, Rose, Rose – it is like Чехоъ. Thank you, Margaret, for everything. And Rolf, & John. Зашумело в голове.

Bernard

When I got back to London I knew that Bernard must be there, getting together equipment for his expedition and seeing anthropologists for advice. But I didn't know where he was staying. I expected him to ring me up or write to me. But he didn't, and I became more and more miserable and anxious. Time was running so short: soon I'd have to return to Cambridge and very soon after

Bernard Deacon, Christmas 1915.

that Bernard would be leaving England. In desperation I confided in an older friend and she managed to discover where Bernard was staying and rang him up. I think she told him that I was unhappy and he ought to come and see me.

He came at once, but there was no ease between us. I was tense and frightened: he was swamped with making arrangements and seeing relevant people. He told me something about his preparations and how he had been to see Malinowski, whom I also knew, for he was a friend of my parents and had often stayed in our house. Malinowski's fieldwork in the Trobriand Islands had enabled him to give Bernard a considerable amount of practical advice.

'He told me how to make arrangements for a native mistress,' Bernard said.

This upset me. 'So what did *you* say?' I asked.

'Oh, I just took notes,' said Bernard.

We spent the evening before my term began together. Coming back late, we stopped outside my parents' house.

'I ought to go in,' I said.

Bernard put his arms round me and kissed me for the first time, but it was a defeated kiss, without zest. He looked down at me very sadly.

'I knew somehow that it wouldn't work with you,' he said.

I went into the house, bewildered, utterly hopeless.

Bernard had promised to come to the station to see me off to Cambridge. We sat in the tea room on the bridge at Liverpool Street station while train after train left for Cambridge. I knew that I should be in trouble with the Newnham authorities if I arrived after eleven, but I couldn't tear myself away from the unhappiness that hung so heavily between us. We seemed to be clamped together in some inexplicable misery. In the end I caught one of the last trains and sat throughout the journey numbed and exhausted, but at least knowing that Bernard would come to Cambridge to see me again before he left.

As soon as he had put me on the train, Bernard went back to the tea room and wrote to me:

Margou – I do hope things aren't too wretched for you owing to tonight. I have been just nothing at all: things seemed to be moving hopelessly in opposite directions and neutralizing. Margou dear, it's so important that you should care about me. I'm sorry to put it so crudely. It is crude in a sense at the moment . . . Do give me something, Margou: I wanted you so much to understand tonight, but everything would persist in following out the same circle over and over again. I couldn't feel you at all. It is so precious, Margou – so worth while . . . Why couldn't I say all this a few minutes ago? . . .

The letter was postmarked 1.15 a.m. and I got it later that same morning. More simple and far less finely tuned than Bernard, I didn't understand, I didn't know what it was that he was asking me to give him, or why he was so unhappy.

He wrote me another letter, unfinished and, I think, unposted.

I see quite clearly that I shall just have to go on alone. I am sure of myself ultimately and I have strength. I must let things gather into their own rhythm . . . It doesn't seem to matter whether we find each other now or later. Perhaps we may never. But it will be all right, whatever it is, I think . . .

Then came a note, scribbled in pencil on a telegraph form:

I can't possibly come to Cambridge tomorrow. It will have to be Tuesday night or early Wednesday morning. I've simply got to finish things first. I wish you were here. I do so want to talk to you. No, be with you. I need quiet so much. So much would come then. I'm so tired. . . . I'll see you. Everything is chiming eleven.

Bernard

He came on Thursday. It was a bright, clear autumn day, glittering, cold and frosty. We walked out to Babraham in a frozen deadlock and only when we had knocked on a cottage door and asked whether they could give us tea did we thaw a little in front of a blazing coal fire. But it was only a physical thawing that brought no real warmth between us. Like little Kay in the fairy story of the Snow Queen, it seemed that splinters of the distorting mirror had pierced our hearts and turned them to ice.

My great Newnham friend, Moris, recently married, had told me that they would be out that evening and had given me a key to their flat, so that Bernard and I could have somewhere to be together quietly. Even there we still had no ease: I was so frightened and there was such urgency, for Bernard would be leaving next day.

It was time for me to go back to College. We both stood up and Bernard said – the words seemed wrenched out of him in despair – 'It's no good, Margou – I don't love you.'

Some deep impulse in me, that I didn't even recognise in myself, made me say 'Never mind. It doesn't matter.'

Suddenly the world was transformed. The lumps of frozen misery that had divided us dissolved, melted away, were gone. Happiness flowed between us, washed over us, was everywhere.

'May I kiss you?' Bernard absurdly asked.

He kissed me very gently on the mouth and we walked out of the flat without speaking. There was no need to speak. My whole being felt utterly changed, my body weightless, my feet scarcely touching the ground. And I knew that Bernard, too, was utterly changed, that we no longer had any doubts about each other or about ourselves. At the gate of the college we parted easily and simply.

Next day Bernard sent me a telegram from Tilbury, where he was embarking: 'Goodbye Margaret   things are tremendously right.'

Bernard wrote to me continuously, both on his journey and then from the New Hebrides. Many of the letters were undated and I'm not sure of their sequence: there were others that were never posted but were sent to me by Dr Haddon after Bernard's death from among his papers, as well as scraps half finished or with pages missing. Bernard's first letter from the ship:

> . . . Words seem so idle and irrelevant now. I don't know what it is
> has been born in the calm and stillness of that inextinguishable joy.
> It is alive in everything in the most marvellous way – loveliness and
> fruitfulness.
>
> We are steaming through a school of dolphins – myriads leaping
> and flashing in the sun. The sea is like glass. Each day since we left
> has been unbelievable beauty. Yesterday we passed the rock of
> Lisbon, distant and clear in the light of the setting sun: not a cloud

in the sky except distant banks, faint and motionless over Portugal.
The sunsets seem to belong to the land of myth and fable – Sinbad
and the Roc and the Phoenix might rise from them and vanish in
the west along the last tracts of fading light. Fuente d'Onores,
Cintra, Badajoz.

My chief cabin-mate is an old ship's captain who has spent his
life trading in the South Seas – he began life on a recruitment
schooner, kidnapping niggers for the plantations in Queensland.
He's got asthma now, and does little else but sit in the bar and drink
with another old skipper he has unearthed from somewhere. He
considers the nigger is a gentleman if you treat him as such –
whatever that may mean.

. . . what can I say to you? I'm quite certain: there is no doubt
anywhere and no fear. I am most terribly sure about myself. And so
glad . . . Malekula is becoming very real. I do so wish you had been
coming. It is so important for us to do things together – and we
could have done that. It may be so fruitful, so deep and lovely.

It is very early in the morning so I have had the deck to myself;
but people are coming up in dozens now. The ship is terribly
crowded.

I didn't leave Cambridge till Friday morning – 7.20 – after all. I
had to sit up nearly all night with Vera. It was more wrong than I
had ever thought, and I could do nothing. But she saw in the end
and, when things had burnt out, the ghastly falsity of all the unreal,
appropriate emotions. We were both rather tired, and it was finished.
I just caught the 7.20 up to town. The grey mists of the morning
were so strange, with a queer happiness in gas works and signal
boxes and shunting engines in the yards. I don't know what part of
me it had all belonged to. Yes, I do – but it seemed so strange that it
should affect anyone beyond me, and above all that it should ramify
into a scene in the early hours of the morning with a mixture of don
Juan and the family doctor: *comédie bourgeoise*. It is strange that
things should have come right only at the very end, when joy came
for the first time with the pure spirit of comedy.

But Bernard was mistaken about Vera. I never met her and I
didn't even know her surname, but very many years later a friend
of mine came across her and he must have mentioned my name,
for she recognised it. She told my friend that she was still deeply

puzzled, that she had never understood what it was that Bernard had been trying to explain to her that night.

On board the S.S. Ormonde
Sunday, August 25th, 1925

. . . I do wish I could be with you – somewhere, anywhere. It is like pitiless fine rain, this drawing apart. Writing is so unreal, so terribly unreal, lending the illusion of movement to quiet and stillness, and holding back desire and vision and the cool, clear welling up of things . . .

We will be in Naples in about an hour. It is very cold, with a tremendous sea running and a high wind. The Mediterranean is an absolutely deserted sea, we passed only one boat off Corsica. Corsica and Elba looked barren and deserted . . .

It is impossible to write in this wind and we are not allowed below till the medical inspection is over . . . Please understand this letter: I'm overwhelmed by environment: wind, and babies, and interruptions.

Naples

I have just finished a lot of letters and am feeling terribly efficient, rather like a businessman. I could sit in a tube in tight striped trousers to be whisked home to say 'Well, my dear' to an *entgegenkommendes* wife. We are steaming into the Bay of Naples. Everything is tremendously alive and young. The wind has dropped, leaving the sky a deep deep blue, pale towards the horizon where hundreds of little white clouds are floating, delicate and rippled like rocks and rivers in Bellini and Mantegna landscapes. There are green wooded heights with castles, like Moussorgsky's lovely piece – but I never played it to you. Margou, why didn't we find each other ever so long ago? There is no piano aboard that I can play – I mean, there is in the 1st class, someone was playing Chopin studies two nights ago, very very well. I'm appallingly romantic. No, I'm not at all really but I like romantic things and places and people. They seem right in an odd sort of way like peasants and miners do at another end of the scale. (I'm feeling terribly feudal at present – at least, society is made up of layers, each with its own proprieties, virtue consists in cultivating one's own proprieties – this is probably because I've started the first part of *Du Côté de chez Swann* again, it is rather like that.)

Proust seems to me very uneven. Sometimes you feel the image is very happy, and you feel you have suddenly broken through to a minute and perfect world in which shades of sense-impression are poised in exquisite proportion. It is like a fantastic Chinese lantern or a miniature pagoda: but you have to pay so dearly for the perfection: so many of the images are tedious and laboured and really incoherent . . . There is one perfect phrase in the first 40 pages . . .

Margou, I must stop. There is tea. The sun is everywhere, on chairs, tables, babies, on a girl's hair, on the white houses of Naples and on the hills.

Goodbye – for a few days.

One of the letters that Bernard had so efficiently written must have been to his friend, W. E. Armstrong, a lecturer in Social Anthropology. I have a fragment of it:

I have been re-reading *Gulliver's Travels* with great joy – particularly the Lilliputians. The Brobdingnagians never appealed to me so much. I'm also ambitiously embarking once more on Proust, but the spectacle of two volumes of *Sodom and Gomorrah* as the reward of patience at the end of the long journey rather appals me.

There is a fancy dress ball of some kind going on. Travelling 3rd is rather trying in some ways – the most irksome being the absence of a table on which one can write comfortably. The writing room is unbearably hot. We have been 18 days on the journey now, & people are beginning to get peevish or randy, according to temperament . . .

s.s. Ormonde
November 6th, 1925

Margou dear – There is such fineness and perfect relation in things: I am separate and definite somehow – I don't know what this marvellous detail and unity means. It is like a cool clear stream flowing in and out: just as if I were near you . . .

[16]

How incredibly good that we are free: it is more worth while than anything I can think of.

I have been so tired of people: it was a kind of impotence, but anything was better than the terrible blindness of 'union' – entangling a unity which simply *exists* in the meaningless stress and strain of a relation so sterile, so useless.

Margaret, thank you so very much, so much, again and again and again. I was terribly blind before, and there was so much fear: ghastly beating at the door, knowing that unless whoever opened it could add his light to mine the darkness would be deeper than before, and the prison more pitilessly confirmed. dear, dear you, I am so terribly thankful.

I'm sorry I wrote from Naples: I didn't understand. There was no drawing apart; it was only because it was Europe still and the closeness seemed to be slipping away every hour. Now everything has gone and we are nearing the equator – quivering, breathless air and the sun burning its way deeper and deeper into the sea; till suddenly each evening you see it hanging motionless over the edge of the sky, before it plunges and vanishes in a pool of light and the stars come tumbling out in thousands.

Nearly everyone is sleeping on deck – the cabins are stiflingly hot – women and children separated from men by an awning. The stars are strange, I don't know them: only away towards the north low over the horizon you can see Capella and Algol in Perseus, Auriger and Cassiopeia.

Third class is very interesting: yesterday Lord & Lady Somebody and their daughter, together with the Captain and officers, came down into 3rd class to distribute prizes, and charmed us with their unaffected bonhomie. An actress from the 1st class (whose name I have forgotten) was also present, and in honour of the occasion we were given iced lemonade and sandwiches for supper instead of cocoa and biscuits, and stood up and cheered Lord & Lady X and the Captain.

On Sundays the Salvation Army, of which we have nearly a platoon on board, holds a prayer meeting morning and evening on deck. I never realized before how much blood (or Blood?) figured in Xtianity. They sing ghastly hymns about it, and preach washing or bathing in it, like Marat (or Robespierre?) in the French revolution. Through it we shall be 'cleansed', but I did not gather how.

[17]

I have been reading *L'Âme enchantée* by Romain Rolland, which an old French lady on the boat has lent me. I saw her husband down the gangway at Toulon, an old gentleman, quite blind. He was a maker of scientific balances and went blind working long hours: they have not enough to live on now and she is going to Australia to try and earn sufficient to keep herself there and him in France: they have lived together 43 years, near Lyons. What an end to life! I like her very much: there was something of *l'Âme enchantée* in their last goodbye. How ghastly the conjunction of age and poverty and uselessness must be and strange that anything can survive it . . .

There was a postcard from Port Said and then a long gap. The next letter was headed Christmas Day, 1925, Lord Howe Island.

Margou dear – I have been silent so long. I don't know why. I've started writing again and again, and each time the futility of it overwhelms me. I seem so terribly far away from you now . . . Cambridge is quite inconceivable. It is in my mind now like one of those strangely tinted postcards you can buy at railway stations. Each scene is like a dim lantern slide, with people moving jerkily and puppet-like, tiny figures across the screen. Then King's chapel has a special slide to itself, with dark, romantic clouds gathering behind it, like Tyrolean scenes a Russian colonel used to show us in his magic lantern. There is a small spot of light and my tutor, Mrs G., the Museum, Great Court, pass across it in silent procession.

I wonder whether you can find Lord Howe Island on the map? It is just a few cliffs standing in the sea and sloping down at the back to white sands and a bowling green – all the islanders play bowls, and are divided into castes forming a social hierarchy according to the percentage of black blood they have in them – quadroons, octoroons etc. There are two or three purely white families who keep aloof from the others – a little aloof.

Industry is entirely on a communistic basis, to a large extent property also. One of the chief exports is the Lord Howe Island palm, used for decorating ballrooms – they are shipped to Sydney and the profits divided on the basis of families etc. and spent for them.

The crew has refused to work on Christmas Day – it is very hot – so we are stuck here till tomorrow. Whale boats came off from the island with lanterns last night to land friends for Christmas-eve parties. There is something queer and unreal about traditional English institutions here – they hound you persistently and tenaciously across the face of the earth. In Sydney there was a huge Christmas shopping rush, with Santa Claus in all the big shops like Harrods, and decorations of snow and holly, people buying surfing costumes and trains packed with trippers going down to the beaches, 102 in the shade.

I had a remarkable historical dream last night. I was in bed with Catherine II (the Great), the lover in favour at the moment. She was of a marvellous softness and whiteness, like a huge feather bed, and astonishingly young and alive for her age. While I lay with her she talked to me with charming brilliance about Diderot and the Encyclopédistes, laughingly about poor old Peter III, amusingly about Princess Dashkova (who was rather a prude) – a rippling succession of *bon mots*. She enjoyed a lover just as she enjoyed coffee after dinner – she could relax, she could confide, she could be affectionate, while I was an unobtrusive stimulus to all these activities. When she had reviewed and dismissed all the topics of the day, she treated me with exceptional kindness and allowed me to withdraw, and I picked my way through long empty corridors with the light of a taper in a silver stick. The whole thing was incredibly real and I could remember nearly every detail when I woke up to find myself a century later at the other side of the world. I wonder whether she did talk to her lovers like that? It seems to me a terribly attractive idea. Did any of them write memoirs? I should think the Orlovs must have done.

I'm sorry to bore you with Catherine. I'm not the least bit a courtier, and she's impossibly incongruous on Christmas-eve in mid-Pacific. The Bolshies found her all dust when they took her jewels, didn't they?

The rest of that letter is missing: the next one, written a few days later – December 28th, 1925 – is headed 'Norfolk Island – Vila – on board s.s. Makambo:

It is a perfect, cloudless day, the sea deep deep blue and alive with long white foam crests. I landed in Norfolk Island yesterday morning from a whale boat – it is very exciting, with a great swell in the bay, and surf breaking against the rocks. The landing place is called the Cascades: there are large pieces of whale strewn about the rocks, and coffee-coloured Tahitian men and boys waiting about with ponies and sulkies by the road up through the cliffs. The island is peopled (you know, I suppose) with descendents of the mutineers of the *Bounty* and the Tahitian women they married. They speak a beautiful English mixed with Tahitian – *wan a' ha* means conceited, *ink no 'ot*=negative, 'I don't think' etc. There was a woman on board returning to her home in the island and I drove up with her through the hills and valleys to an old house hidden behind peach trees and orange bushes and palms. The island is loveliness itself.

Feathery pines on the hills, like a frieze against the sky, and steep, fertile valleys, with lemon orchards hidden by blue convolvulus and hanging bougainvillaeas like lava flowing down the sides, blossomy frosted flame trees, sweet smelling oaks in flower (not our English oak), olives among the rocks, a creeper called Samson's hairs, & the Alsophilas, tree ferns, rising above the bed of the valley like starfish opening to the sun – : teeming, silent growth everywhere. Out behind the house there are scarlet splashes of hibiscus, lovely flowers: I had breakfast there, and then lunch – or dinner – with baked sweet potatoes and yams, and passion-fruit and peaches, endless peaches, – you squash them underfoot as you walk. The island is divided into 25 acre lots & originally there were 29 mutineer families – half-Tahitian, half-English. Each family had a 25 acre lot. When a son married, an unused lot was portioned off for him. Now there are only 7 or 8 of the old families surviving – everyone on the island is either Christian, or Quintal, or McCoy, etc., the names of the original mutineers. They have made their own laws, their own customs regulations. There is practically no export trade – some lemons are exported, sufficient to buy kerosene etc. from the ship when she calls. They make hats from a creeper growing down the cliffs, carts from pine wood. No intoxicants are allowed to be drunk. There are no pests & no venomous reptiles on the island.

We are steaming almost due north now, past the Isle of Pines and Maré, in the Loyalty Islands, into the tropics again – we reach Vila on New Year's Eve. I tranship again there into the *Makatea* for South West Bay. I feel stranger and stranger about Malekula now that it's so tantalizingly close.

Bernard Deacon with his parents in Russia.

I had been planning to try and join Bernard somehow or other, and I had written to tell him so. Now the letter went on: 'Margou dear – you're not really coming out, are you? I've got . . .' and there was a list, two pages long, of the stores he was taking, ending with 'I've also got a tent and things, so you could almost stay with me without bringing out a great deal.' The letter continued:

I have been working quite hard the last three weeks in Melbourne and Sydney – going round to various people's private collections and making sketches etc., buying provisions, chemicals for photography, gun and ammunition etc. – I seem to have met and seen an unending number of people – I was booked every day for lunch and dinner – most of them are connected with the islands or with anthropology in general – they matter in that sense. I stayed most of the time at Sydney in College at the University – it was heart-rending to be imitating the worst features of Cambridge from morning to night – incidentally, everyone got up and stamped and cheered the first night I went into Hall with the Warden.

'Macquarie Street, flanked with symmetrical macrozanias' – it suddenly flew into my head. Why? I stayed there in Sydney with an anti-Freudian (I think pro-Jungian) mental specialist. One of his patients – a woman – used to walk with God, like Enoch, waiting to be caught up to heaven. Poor, wasted thing.

I sit on the right hand of the Captain at dinner. He tells me gory tales of kanakas and Malekula . . . According to him, you can live on nothing in the islands provided you are a good bridge player – it is the universal pastime of the New Hebrides – even apparently among 'civilized' natives.

I'm in the middle of *War and Peace* – I've decided that a good deal of the first two parts *is* dull – but how hopelessly, unforgettably perfect the wolf hunt and the sleigh drive to the country house of the M—s and Natasha – Natasha, strange funny youthful Natasha, cool and fresh and childlike and unconscious that she is a beautiful wilful passionate woman. No, that's not Natasha: it's hopelessly not you: dear Natasha! it would be wicked to describe you: you just *are*. And Pierre – how like him Serge Nabokoff was – Pierre, large, round, true, dissipated, clumsy, profound, capable Pierre – if only there were more Pierres! And Moscow and the Rostoffs: and old Prince Bolkonsky – what calm restrained, superb artistry – like the greatest of Rembrandt – don't you think Tolstoi is like Rembrandt, and Stravinski like Botticelli – I hate analogies? Bolkonsky is marvellous, one of the greatest, most perfect of Tolstoi's creations – hewn out of light and shade, immobile in the last rays of his setting sun, poised, complete, vividly, indelibly massive – surpassing grandeur – superb old Bolkonsky – and Andrei Bolkonsky? I don't know. Andrei puzzles me. I can understand him as *someone else*, but I cannot for one moment *be* Andrei. Existence of his kind seems to belong to a different dimension or constitution of things. He holds together differently and I always feel some of him is stuffed – a little – e.g. his behaviour in early parts at the front. Why is Speranski so almost spitefully caricatured? He was not worth it and he did very fine work for Russia – his codification of the laws was in its way a masterpiece. Tolstoi cannot believe in cold, clever people who work methodically and hard and do a great deal.

I'm incredibly happy, Margou. I don't know what I am to say to you. Nothing, nothing . . . It is imperishably good that I know you – but there is a completeness lacking – I feel severed by seas and skies and great tracts of country from something that belongs to me very immediately and acutely – like a bird might feel a wing . . . The joy is *one*, somehow: it has made some things grow tiny and imperceptible points, scarcely discernible in all the great new spaces – it is rather like Revelation, but without fantastic women and horses and trumpets . . . It is strange how letters grow to a pattern, with a *divertissement à deux* at the end. I'm sorry, I'm suddenly feeling old and incredulous.

Dear you: it's horribly long.

Bernard

Margou, – no, I won't say it: goodbye.

on board s.s. Makambo

Margou dear – is all this Malekula really right and good? It is so fantastically irrelevant somehow – and I feel so much time going on it, this endless, endless time, great corridors and passages of it, leading nowhere.

. . . I can't write at all today – do you remember – oh, all sorts of things – having tea by ourselves in a firelit room at the end of your house in Holland Park – there was something so right between us then, and I thought, ridiculously, how could you put salt on its tail?; but then it passed.

It is morning, and New Year's day: we are in Vila harbour: I've just been across to the residency in a launch: there's a letter from you . . . I need all my energy, every moment now – I'm sorry, that's all disconnected and meaningless – I'm sorry – today I'm full of a queer joy, and heaps and heaps of pain has vanished, it is so cool and clear after the unremitting pain of knowing again and again, hour after hour that you are not there, that you can't possibly be there . . . I want to be near you and then you would understand it all without my speaking. If only this stuffy little cabin could be Moris's room.

I wanted to chuck up everything and join Bernard in Malekula but I didn't know how I was to do it. For one thing, I hadn't the money for the journey and my parents would certainly not help me in what they'd consider a crazy – and indeed, immoral – enterprise. Time was moving more swiftly for me, surrounded by friends and all the interests of Cambridge life, than it was for Bernard in his isolation. I wanted very much to be with him but my longing didn't have the same urgency: I didn't doubt that somehow or other, before long, we'd be together. Meanwhile I dropped Moral Science, which I'd been reading, and started on a Russian course which seemed to bring me closer to Bernard. He was delighted when I told him about this, and flatteringly – but wrongly – assumed that I would have some of his own linguistic brilliance and his appetite for work.

I'm incredibly glad that you're reading Пчмкин and understanding him. Do read some things of Tyutchev's too. If you can find a book of his poems, I'd be very very glad of one – in fact, I don't know how, I don't seem to have brought any Russian poetry, & feel an unbearable lack sometimes. Oh, yes, and Fet. But you'll know them all by now. It's a lovely language.

And sometimes after that he would add a little piece in Russian to his letters.

Bernard was now in Malekula, with his base at South West Bay.

The steamer only called about once a month and letters to and from England would often take as long as six weeks.

Sometime in March

The steamer has turned up – here I have only half finished letters. Dear, it is useless, I can't write. It seems to drag down and weigh down what I feel into something wooden and unreal – I just lose heart to go on. There must be letters in the steamer from you. It is in the bay now, a tiny speck, swinging at anchor outside the reef . . . What else am I to say? There is a queer, uncontrolled loveliness rushing through everything, and I cannot stay it. Perhaps it is the steamer – I'm sorry – I'm hopelessly overcome by things. It is cool and alive after the heavy, dense heat . . .

South West Bay
end of March

Margou dear – it is grey dawn and I am sitting down writing hurriedly. I was wakened when it was scarcely light by the echoing of the steamer's siren through the Malekulan hills and valleys (it is all hills and valleys) – it is a terrifying, uneasy sound – you are suddenly paralysed that so many weeks have gone. It is the only real measure of time here – I can see it coming up into the Bay now, a wavy ribbon of black smoke. The old captain has left and I will not know the new one. The crew is native – Tanna boys with scarlet lavalavas – one died of dysentery last time it called & they had to hold up the steamer to bury him.

A native has just brought me up two letters – sickening ones – one from my bank in Cambridge, who have been stupid and sent only £30 instead of £100 – however, that's all right – the other an account from Vila for kerosene, cigarettes, mouth organs and pipes, amounting to £11, which is utterly preposterous – it shouldn't be more than £4 . . . It's a nuisance, I hate it all. 'I beg to acknowledge . . . it is also noted that you wish . . . the amount standing to your credit . . .' One is absolutely at the mercy of one company here – Burns Philp (South Sea) Ltd – their steamer comes every five weeks, & you either buy from them or go without – quinine, bandages, matches, rice, milk, everything – and they just charge whatever they like. And in a climate like this you cannot go without civilization suddenly and adopt native life. Actually I should say the natives are much weaker and more diseased than the whites – they are constantly down with malaria, even though they take quinine, and yaws is universal. I had malaria badly about three weeks ago, but it hasn't recurred, and I think is not going to. It's a wretched thing, anyway.

I'm so sorry, Margou, this letter has suddenly developed into a dirge. Thank you for sending the Gorki etc. – they came last time: I'm so sorry but I really haven't looked at them – instead I've been reading an absurd book by Trollope, about life in some cathedral town in England. Even Tolstoi seems a little shallow & unreal here – incongruous. Malekula is so real that you can only read things that are outside you and leave the days clear and unaffected – I've been reading the New Testament in French, which I disliked before. I can quite understand the gospels appealing to the natives: they are wonderful things . . .

There is so much else, but I can do no more than scribble desultorily, because it is all so meaningless. Things here have a tremendous vividness and power of their own, but it all crumbles if you try to put it in relation with anything outside – and *you* have no relation with Malekula, except a very mystic sort of one – I'm sure you think Malekula a myth or nightmare . . . I feel as if I'm going round and round a bean-stalk of contradictions, only there is no ogre at the top. How is Mrs G? I must write to her, and to Peter [Mrosovsky] – he would be lovely on Malekula – it's a little peterish.

dear you – this mustn't go on any longer

goodbye

P.S. I have been brought a letter – asking me to tea in Newnham – oh, God! Daedalus!

South West Bay
Malekula
[May]

. . . Sometimes, after rain, my island seems fantastically close, off Dover somewhere, or in the Channel, and I'm absurdly happy again. Then suddenly I'm back in Malekula again, with the heavy, heavy heat. It makes you feel as weak as a babe.

We have Tonkinese here, imported by the French from Cochin China: they fawn on you for laudanum, which is difficult to get.

. . . This burden of time, leaden-footed time, in so strange, so unlikely a world – can't you feel corals and coconuts almost on the page? Shady beaches, with a cool translucent light and the murmur of bees. There is a strange quality in the light, it is mobile and part of things – *je ne sais quoi*. Everything is a little inconsequent, a little contradictory: I have a bit of fever today and it is like a veil over the world. Yet the earth is pleasant enough . . . I have finished a mass of notes to Haddon today, and a letter to Armstrong, and now there is nothing but the sense of an overwhelming futility, and acquiescence in months of patient work – and I am so tired of acquiescence, so very tired. Please understand, Margou – but it will be weeks & weeks & miles & miles of ocean routes and all the mechanism of civilization before 'two people are completely present to one another', as Haldane says we are all to be some day when Daedalus comes into his own. I don't know why, I am fundamentally interested in science——I'm sorry, I was suddenly changing round to something else in the last sentence. It had very little to do with anything.

S.W.Bay
Sometime in May
(about 14th)

I'm away from S.W.Bay and the steamer is passing, the only chance of sending anything. I hope to goodness this catches it. Life has become one ceaseless concentration on the immediate object – the climate accounts for it partly. I'm down on the south coast at present, living in a yam house, will be up at SWB in a few days' time. I wish there were two of me, it is fearfully difficult to do any decent intellectual work with the constant pressure of physical existence. I haven't had fever for some time though I seem to have done lamentably little in the free interval.

Margou, *do* believe in things: it's a bare statement but I cannot write more.

It would have been lovely with you.

[27]

South West Bay
June 1926

. . . it is a strange tropical autumn here – a cool wind sweeping fitfully through tracts of immobile, intolerable heat. I have spent the morning in a dispersed desultory sort of way trying to piece together the work of the past four months and realizing again and again with a sort of mild panic how lamentably inadequate it is. At one or two points there has been a sudden vision of what the whole might be like, a sense of the movement of everything as marvellously living and an uncontrollable joy in it – and then suddenly there is this now constantly recurring, overwhelming depression, a sudden draining of intellect and will, by which alone it is possible to live here. There is nothing in this forgotten world to which I can act as a whole, except this vision of a consummation and a unity – and yet it is what I must most constantly doubt. It is so easy, in this strange heat, for very weariness of flesh to rest content with something imperfect and obscure, a prostitution of the desire of the inmost spirit towards – what? the possibility of truth? It is a strange love. You are so much more than a possibility: perhaps it is just that . . . the burden of this separation is intolerable, and the strength to continue it a weariness.

It seems to me more than ever important that we should do something together: I feel it the one inevitable thing, and utterly good: so good that it scarcely matters where we are together. We have perfect freedom and shut ourselves in prisons. '*Ne vous conformez point au siècle présent, mais soyez transformés par le renouvellement de votre esprit.*' There is a perfection of spirit in Pascal and St Paul which seems to me sometimes to be the only ultimate meaning in life, as far as we have yet lived. I have an immense distrust of solutions in other directions: perhaps I am innately conservative in this affection for the past yet I have a very great belief in the value of science.

It has always seemed to me that the 'decadents' – the French particularly, I know little about the others, possibly people like Sologub, and Tchekhov, as a philosopher – realized a new value, made possible by the perception of the meaning of science, towards which people like Haldane are beginning, rather heavily, to move (among the scientists). The decadents were intensely preoccupied with coordinating experience, perhaps the Cézanne people would

[28]

say with making its form 'significant', it really doesn't matter what symbols you chose. The balance of scientist and artist and human being in Tchekhov is perhaps the most perfect life in this renewing of the spirit. I wish Tchekhov had written something like the *Pensées* or the epistles of St Paul: he had the clarity, the justness of phrase & the profound wisdom.

But Margou this is all nothing while we are prisoners ... it seems to me overwhelmingly urgent that we should be together, and that we should do something, to the end, together. This world is hopeless; it must be in Europe somewhere, Russia or Serbia perhaps. I haven't been in Russia, for ten years – no, nearly ten. It is the only place I shall ever believe in, I suppose: we are like angels and as remote from humanity: you can love English people but they are so difficult to believe in. What rot I'm writing. I have no life here, but a desire to finish it: the very strength to go on is weakness: it is bitter.

... what is all this covering of paper with tiny black marks, absurd like a Chinese convention? There is a Chinaman here, in the Bay, entirely uncommunicative: the steamer brought me a Chinese newspaper once which should have gone to him: I should have liked to have read it, but it seemed all utterly illogical, so I took it down to him and he appeared overjoyed. He is very polite. Once he had fever, and grew delirious.

Margou dear, I cannot forget you, nor the joy that is in me because of you: this conflict is intolerable. You see, I am most terribly interested in ethnology, in what I want to try and do, but it seems all at right angles to this new life that is within me. One should be part of the other, but now they can't be. Courage and patience and all those stoical virtues are merely a futile prolonging of the disharmony. Margou, if you get this letter, please write to me about it. Margou, I can't give up until I have finished here, another six months at least. I wish to God things would move faster, but there are blocks and hindrances every day. I don't know whether you can realize how acute the conflict is: the only way I can escape is to forget, and then the thing becomes a greater mess. The only way I can bring any harmony into being is by believing in a wholly fictitious courage: – I hate and loathe courage. The only solution is to live entirely in the intellect and will. It all seems so irrelevant, so

[29]

hopelessly insignificant beside what we found. And then suddenly I am hopelessly fond of – what? the possibility of unravelling things: it must seem foolish to you beyond words: I am so sorry, Margou, but I cannot help it. Margou dear, if you tell me to leave and come back, I think I would. Do tell me something. It seems so absurd that you and this other desire should be linked in conflict. There was this same absurdity when I came to England from Russia – the same conflict of desires that made me alternate between physics and Russian and ethnology at Cambridge. I feel if I could only go to Russia, or to Serbia perhaps, with you, it might resolve things. Perhaps there are lectureships or something of the kind at universities like Харьков or Одесса, or Moscow. If I could be with you then it would be freedom and joy. But even if we could go to Russia together – it is a place of such vast potentialities that there are thousands of things we could do. I doubt whether I could lecture in Russian, in any case, until I had lived there again. If only I could unite you with this strange belief – with no foundation except in this inmost spirit – in *something* in Russia. It all seems an incongruity, but I have an essential belief in these miracles; – anyway, Russia is another world. It is this Malekula which is so absurd: it has connection only through ethnology, and ethnology and physics and all those things are only one aspect of what I am, so Malekula has scarcely any relation at all, and yet I am imprisoned and fettered by its irrelevancy. It seems to me terribly important *now soon* to work out some kind of harmony . . . I don't know what your will is, except between us. I had a letter from Haddon, from which apparently the Sydney thing will be filled before I'm finished. Sydney, of course, is only the solution of economic necessity. My relation to Australia would be *evil* except through the aboriginals, and the whole thing would be inevitably a half solution, though that is better than none.

I wish to God you had come into relation with me when I was doing Russian in Cambridge. I wish I had known Rolf better then, but he was moving and acting in a direction which must have seemed utterly out of relation to anything I was doing. What is Rolf doing now? I was always sorry, foolishly I suppose, that he had to work in that intolerable 'cadre' of Cambridge – bright, centreless young men, and all the mutual admiration coteries and cliques and groups with their figures. What has become of S. and all that group with their airy buggery? What was it that made them preserve that tradition with the childish, scrupulous care that an old general preserves the decorations of his years of active service. I cannot conceive that they got an atom of joy out of the cult: I think S. always feared I might really be homosexual, and turn out to be a bull in the china-shop. S.R. was, but mildly and genteelly. I always had the sensation of having been at a nightmarish play after an evening at S's – a play without motives or relevancy. I loved to be with Goard then: I was always profoundly happy with Goard: his room was the only place in Cambridge that I loved to go to. But Goard was a genius, with his powers destroyed by the war, and lack of means, and Cambridge, and other things too. He wrote one quartet, magically fresh and lovely, a marvellous, delicate thing. I don't think it was ever performed, except the first section once in a room in Neville's Court . . .

Margou dear, the loveliness of you is within me and about me: there has been rain while I wrote, and the scent of flowers fresh after the rain.

If only it were not so long, so terribly long . . .

Later.

Still no steamer, thunder and torrential rain all round, and a big westerly sea coming in. I had a low fever all the forenoon, but it is gone now and I am calm, just sweating gently. Today at tea-time there was a big earthquake shock, and the ground is still moving at intervals. The whole thing is queer, and rather terrifying. It is the worst we've had, I think Ambrym must be active again: on dark nights you can sometimes see the red reflections of it in the sky. There was a famous eruption there in 1913, when the sea rushed in and formed a lake where the Mission Hospital stood, and the lava poured down to the sea. The islands are really coral fringes round the peaks of submerged, extinct volcanoes (there are only three active now) – a great volcanic chain running from New Zealand to Japan. In some ways I should like to remain here for ever, remaking myself. It is a magnificent setting for a play, a desolate, timeless paradise.

But to the natives, of course, just their home: passing through a village at sundown, they are cooking their evening meal (breadfruit) at their fires, the women separately, the men together in the club-house, the blue smoke curling up lazily through the overshadowing

Bernard Deacon with his parents, 1920.

branches of some great banyan-tree. The names of their villages are picturesque – 'Under the Banyan-tree', 'The Place of Red Earth', 'The Hidden House', 'The House of Peace', 'The House of Death', 'The Sacred Place by the Sea'. The life of the native is much more constrained, convention-ridden and ceremonial than ours – (mine or yours). One man of my acquaintance did not marry a girl he wanted very much, for fear that he might forget the rules of conventional respect towards parents-in-law when in presence of her father or mother. These complexes are very real to the native: it would be a happy hunting ground for the psychologists, especially Freudian. And as for magic! it is what 'logic' or 'common sense' is for us, a thing unthinkable to deny, implicit, inevitable, universal. Far more attention needs to be paid to it than has been in the past by ethnologists. I have great respect for Malinowski in this direction.

It would be a wonderful world to live in, here, were it not that the natives are the last survivors of a dying people – dysentery, ulcers of all sorts, measles, whooping cough (fatal diseases here), opthalmia, tetanus – there is scarcely a strong man or woman among them. Even malaria they stand much worse than I do, with all the quinine and empirin they take. They have to be filled up with medicines to keep them alive – Neo-Kharsivan especially. I think probably the conventional savage is a myth: there are simply backward peoples. The solution, that is to say, has to be sought forward, not behind. Probably during the next 50 years civilization will have penetrated to every area of the world, & we shall then see what races have gone under & which are going to survive as competitors in the evolution of mankind. We have a long start in the race; & should eliminate a good many: e.g. the New Hebrides are almost bound to go. One price these isolated races have paid for their isolation is a terrible susceptibility to diseases against which we have apparently innoculated ourselves – I mean, measles & so on, ? tuberculosis, syphilis too – 'nous ne civilisons pas, nous syphilisons' as a Roman Catholic priest here said to me, with much truth. Paradoxically, studying the natives has stimulated a great interest in the most advanced civilization – the American(U.S.A.). You can scarcely realize, till you get outside Europe, how dominant America and American civilization is in the world today – e.g. in Australia, which is already more American than English. The achievement of places like America, and even Australia, is tremendous. With England, the supremacy

has nothing to do with you. Spanish influenza has wiped out whole villages in Santo, Pentecost & Malekula, one might say districts. As for work, I despair & despair again. Against this overwhelming hopeless atmosphere it is almost insupportable to labour. It is difficult at times not to feel bitter, really it is a wretched atmosphere to do a first piece of work in and takes quite 50% off the value of anything you do, 'the men who knew are dead' is its eternal refrain. I have to piece together scraps that when Layard was here were a whole that could be seen and witnessed and gone through in actual experience.

Even then it simply didn't occur to me that Bernard himself might be in any danger: after all, he was a white man and immune from most of the diseases that were killing the natives. I didn't recognise or understand the extent to which recurrent fevers and sores, the debilitating climate, the sheer difficulties of his physical existence and his doubts and despairs about his work were undermining his health. I hadn't, of course, asked him to come back, for I knew that to do so would only have increased the conflict of his desires – and in any case, I was still hoping to join him. So it seemed to me just a matter of time before we would be together 'to the end', as Bernard had written. That the end might be so near was inconceivable.

I had left Cambridge and was trying to find a way of getting to the New Hebrides. I had discovered John Layard's address and, although I had never met him, I went to his flat unannounced and rang the bell. When he opened the door, I nearly retreated, for he looked so forbidding, dishevelled and distraught. But when I had explained that I was a friend of Bernard's and wanted some information about Malekula, he asked me in, saying, 'He's an absolutely marvellous chap'. It was the start of a long friendship between us.

At that period John was painfully fighting his way out of the breakdown that had followed his work in the islands. He felt that everything – and everybody – was conspiring to prevent him from writing the book for which he had amassed such splendid material and that he was floundering in a morass of misery from which he couldn't extricate himself. Yet through all the then disorder of his life there shone that strain of human warmth and generosity that was to lead to his recovery and his very special insights. It had been this capacity for love, I think, that had enabled him to get so close an understanding of the natives of the New Hebrides and had given him the zest to join in their dances and songs. He danced some of the dance steps for me, and sang some of the songs – the leaf and the fruit – the refrain and the verse, and introduced me to the delights of pidgin English. But it was too long since he had been in Malekula for him to be able to give me any useful practical advice.

In mid-June Bernard had written that he was soon going up to Lambumbu on the north-west coast, where he would be rather cut off, for the steamer didn't call there and he'd have to get letters through as best he could. Some time in July he wrote briefly:

> I've just returned from three days in the bush to find a trader here with a post – or some of it – for me – he's the first 'white' I've seen for – what? I suppose six weeks. He's leaving in a few hours and I've asked him to come and have supper, so I'll have to get some ready – I've got used to living on native puddings, breadfruit, various birds I shoot & so on –
> Sorry, can't finish this. There's a fragment of a letter I began will put it in. A strong gale is coming into the bay & the trader is leaving before nightfall. So sorry . . .

The fragment read:

> It is Sunday – at least according to the natives – so I've knocked off work and am cooking yams and soaking clothes ready for washing & getting an (unnamed) bird cleaned for supper. Everything has changed utterly and completely since I came up here, away from S.W. Bay. – I'm absurdly happy, and hopelessly fond, in some sudden and inexplicable way, of the natives – whether it is any better for anthropology – ridiculous word – God only knows. I'm entirely alone now, and vastly, inconceivably happier. It is lovely country up here, great open plains of deep, soothing bamboo grass, like corn fields. The only troublesome pests are rats. I am living in an old, disused mission house, near the road leading into the village. It is a mat skirt area, the women wear them – stained bright red and yellow – round their middles, & on their head after marriage

(their father-in-law may not see the top of their head): sometimes also they throw one of these mats round their neck & over their breast, like a shawl. The men, as everywhere in Malekula, just wear the penis strapped up the stomach in front.

Lambumbu
N.W. Malekula

Margou – I have been ill, and for the first time today feel nearly my normal strength back. There has been a great epidemic through the islands – apparently Spanish flu, with a very high death rate, 400 on Pentecost and many here, one they have just buried and another late last night; they have to bury them immediately after death here. It is all very tragic, a leap forward again to the laying waste of the New Hebrides . . .

I have learnt one lesson from it – that it is essential if you're going to live in the tropics never to let your strength go down – knock off immediately – feed up and go steady till you do get it back. In a cooler climate where there is no fever, dysentery etc. you can run for a long time on a tired body, gradually getting back strength, but here unless you take steps quick you go lower & lower and then a bout of fever that you can't get rid of practically breaks you down altogether.

I miss very much not being able to discuss any of my work with anyone – the constant return to oneself & attempt to criticize oneself is very enervating. Moreover, I have really very little idea of what others have done here – Layard in '13, Rivers at the same time, then Barnard in 1921 or so, & Humphries. Except for a short very general paper by Rivers, none of this work is yet printed, except, I think, Humphries, as I heard from a friend in Sydney that 'some Humphries' has brought out a book on the New Hebrides. My own work I am in the most complete despair about – both quality & quantity. I am constantly trying to frame some general theory of New Hebrides' culture; really it has been investigated pretty thoroughly, by able men – Codrington, Rivers, Speiser, Layard, Barnard, Humphries – and surely if anywhere here's the chance for ethnology to show what it can arrive at in the way of theory. Rivers' theory I begin to find a hindrance, I was brought up on it at Cambridge, and now it clogs me: on every page I want to cry out 'But there's so many other things!' – and in lots of it I am very much puzzled to know what Rivers really thought about certain things – whether he was aware of particular difficulties, whether he *regarded* them as difficulties. More particularly I want to know what Barnard thinks of Rivers' ideas. There must be more coordination of ethnological work in the field – it's useless letting people just float out & grope in the dark where they want. By all means as much freedom as possible, but in every area of the world the current immediate problems should be worked out & stated as clearly as possible, continuously by each worker. For in most ethnological work at present theories are principally useful in giving sets of problems: the coordination is really very piecemeal. If I get another chance of ethnological field work, I'm going to take an area chosen to test as many problems and theories as possible. Also, what I spoke to Haddon about on several occasions, it is most awfully necessary for, say, the Anthropological Institute, or a Committee of all the various English, German, French & American Institutes, to produce a *reference book* with maps of *distributions* of all the more prominent cultural elements.

As it is, you have to wade through masses of literature to find, for example, every place where incision or circumcision is practised. It's absurd & impossible. One *must* have something better – a definite reference book of ethnological distributions, with annual appendices for additional discoveries. The Germans have I think done a lot of work in this direction, but it is scattered about in *Beitragen* & *Mittheilungen* & what not, & half of it seems to be unknown or disregarded in England. Even then, they disregard the social organization aspect.

Think of having, in Europe, to go through every Parish Magazine & religious periodical to determine the distribution of Protestantism, Roman Catholicism, Greek Orthodoxy, the Uniate Church, Judaism etc. That's the sort of state of affairs in ethnology. One *must* have a cyclopaedia of distributions. The very compilation of one might suggest a dozen theories, and one could refer to it immediately to check theories like Perry & Smith's, which slur over gaps & by selecting here and there, distort the actual complexity. At present, to check & correct them, you have to wade through practically the whole literature of ethnology & travel.

I saw in Sydney a paper by Professor Griffith-Taylor, of Sydney

University, about the diffusion of culture in the Pacific in which
there was a map of distributions on which, by using references of
the type 'occurs in the Northern New Hebrides', 'is characteristic
of the Melanesians' & so on, Malekula was lurid with serpent cults,
sun-mythology, couvade & goodness knows what. Yet if there were
a cyclopaedia of distributions, no one would be able to do this kind
of thing without being at once detected & exposed. Every awkward
occurrence or non-occurrence would be set down, & by reference to
the maps etc., it would be possible at once to appraise the value of
'diffusionist' theories. But most important it would help vastly in
research, both academic & field work. It would also be very useful
to administrators of large areas – e.g. a man sent out to be Commissioner for the Solomons or the New Hebrides even, would see at a
glance what different groups & cultures he had to deal with, as a
geologist looks up a section of England on the geological survey. Of
course the cyclopaedia would have to go into detail – e.g. the
distribution of different types of clothing & so on, nose ornaments –
then things like secret societies, line of descent, clan organization,
types of underworld etc.

Questionnaires would be sent out to missionaries, govt. officials
etc. to fill in the gaps, the whole thing mapped out like the great
Star Catalogues, sections allotted to countries & so on. Of course I
can do nothing. It needs to be taken up by, say, the committee of the
Anthropological Institute.

It seems to me so overwhelmingly urgent that I don't know why
it hasn't been done.

There is another unfinished letter from Lambumbu:

. . . It is just after dawn. It has been a night of sleepless horror and
misery, till the first faint light of day came – Margou, I was so near
you then, simply and utterly unconscious of myself except as with
you . . . it was joy and peace and calm and utter utter loveliness,
welling up and bursting and transfusing everything . . . again and
again there is the overwhelming longing at least to write to you, but
it is so bitter, defeating itself and making me hate myself, making
me something loathsome I am not. There is something in me that I
am that is terribly living and beautiful, so irreducible, the only
meaning I can ultimately give myself, that to deny is to acknowledge

something that I also am that is hideous beyond words . . . that's all wrong, somehow; it's again part of that hideous self: I can't get away from it. It all reduces to being together with you again, simply, as the only meaning . . . if you could be here for five minutes, one minute, half a minute, I could start again weighing out the aching timelessness of days and hours in this unreal world till in some miracle I found myself again in Tilbury Dock – in Naples or Port Said even – anywhere in the Northern Hemisphere – Vladivostock would seem quite close. The only privacy, the only remnant of Europe here, is thought. The publicity of native life is at times maddening. I have been here about 3 months now. There is no white man here, nor does any steamer ever call. There are times of very great depression, especially if one is sick, since all the natives can do, with all the good will in the world, is to gather round and look at you and, blessed moment, go. This sounds quite unlike the 'sympathetic understanding' of the native that anthropologists say one should have. It seems to me fundamentally wrong to 'approach' natives in any way, sympathetic or other. If you live among them any time you soon realize that you are far more dependent on them than they are on you and, if they really offer to accept you as a member of the community, the stress of give and take in the daily life in it soon leaves little room for any attitude except in your rare private moments – you come in for your share of censure, ridicule, chaff, affection, help as any other man, and return what you get. In one's clear moments of private sanity it seems a nightmarish experiment, rather like a public school, I imagine. Romanticism, science, 'values', history, love – of all these necessities of European life they are quite innocent. The line drawn between decency and indecency differs from our conventions – in many ways there is resemblance to France & Russia. A small boy will give a realistic imitation of copulation in public, but it would be indecent and suggestive to point out to a woman that there was a cockroach or a piece of mud on her skirt. The native is essentially a villager and agriculturalist, but he has a wider 'county' or 'district' life which corresponds to our national life since it is that of the whole social group. The Christian converts, a small band, correspond in function and temper to the (idealistic) social revolutionaries of the Bakunin type in Europe – they are out for the destruction and reconstruction of native society. Queerly enough, the only white men revolutionaries

I have come across here, among traders etc. are all on the side of die-hard conservatism in everything concerning native life & against the Xtian innovators. They want all native customs preserved *en bloc*. Personally my sympathies go more to the Christians but they sadly lack funds and backing. I expect Haddon, as a staunch conservative, would condemn such an attitude. In his last letter of May 15th, he says he's got my first batch of notes which is 'wonderful' & that 'You're working on quite the right lines'. He says that there's nothing for me in England & the best thing is for me to try for the Sydney job which, however, he thinks a certain Williams, an Australian-born will get. So far as I can see, when I land in Sydney I won't have funds to carry me home, so I'll *have* to get something there.

At present I'm very depressed about my work. I've got to a stage when it should be mainly 'psychological' I suppose, 'social psychology' or something like that, but I have no training in method and don't know really what one tackles and how. E.g., if you were set down to study the 'sociology' or 'social psychology' of an English village, how would you go at it? Write a sort of novel and then extract theories from it which you'd test out as far as possible by creating 'situations'? It seems a bastard science somehow. Why don't psychologists come and study primitive peoples? You would have quite different sets of types and complexes & what not & from the comparative study of such sets might get some general principles. E.g. here there must be strong complexes corresponding to a man's relation to his mother's brother's wife, with its inhibitions and desires, to his parents-in-law, also round the relation of chief to subsidiary wife (wives). There is infant betrothal, Lesbianism, male homosexuality raised to the rank of an organized male monogamy, with incest taboos between males, concomitant jealousies, insignia (like marriage rings) for ♂ 'husband' & 'lover' etc. Moreover, as white man you have access everywhere. I wish we had been together here: it would have been a great deal easier, two, than one. Also, my interest in natives is too general – in fact, in people as a whole – I don't react spontaneously to them as a person, except rarely. It is only the realization that something I know in myself is known by another that may suddenly – what? – waken me to him. I don't know. Otherwise I may know him but he is relevant only in relation to others. I'm sorry, all this is very dull, I'm not a bit interested . . .

[41]

Margou dear, if I ever succeed in doing any decent work – I wish I could be sure of myself – I would like to do something, in the nature of research, something I believe profoundly to be critical & of value, with you – if we can find a common field somewhere . . .

The day has burst in all its white heat – for two months now there has been no drop of rain, the streams are dry, everywhere no water, no water. I drink dew, a little condenses evening and morning on the roof and trickles down into the tank. Destroying white heat.

3 or 4 days later.

A sudden burst of rain, everything drinking it up greedily, the world is incredibly lovely again, very green and quiet, shady, the heat gone. Very lovely Malekula can be sometimes. I was perhaps unjust to it at first – I had a good bit of fever then, the last month or two it has finished, in fact altogether I'm very well – only sores are a trouble, but I bandage them decently. I very much like this world in its quiet. I think I am getting to love it suddenly, more and more. I see much more than I did before. I think you would love it very much too, but not at first. I think your body has to change somehow first, before life becomes natural. At first you are living with an 'English' body in a tropical climate, & it is a misfit.

The Missionary turned up yesterday on his 'rounds' – like parish visiting in England – *just*: & I suppose this [letter] will go by him. I have suffered more from Xtianity, perhaps, than anything, I'm sorry, as I had no bitterness against it before, & much love.

Do you remember a conversation we once had in which you mentioned something about educating children? No, I did, I think it turned out I was wrong. It occurred to me today. I was thinking whether my reaction to children agreed with what I thought about them. I have put up a swing here – a thing apparently previously unknown. They swing very clumsily. In fact, altogether they're very awkward & unsupple – reminding one of shambling gorillas at times, especially when they put on tight trousers . . .

[*undated*]

It is very late, about midnight: I haven't been able to get to sleep on account of the rats. They are perfectly terrible just now, eating

Bernard Deacon c. 1923.

clothes while you sleep in them. Unfortunately I have nothing but a trap to destroy them with. One night I caught three with the trap and killed one with a stick. I suppose it is October now. I have been living here alone the last – what? – three or four months now. I mean, alone in the house. Hullo, there's an earthquake tremor. This house is so ricketty, being built on piles, long disused and riddled with white ants, that the least shake sets it going like a pram.

It is very difficult, in more or less complete isolation, to gain sufficient stimulus for work. I find I have to build it up internally, by theorizing. Almost any hypothesis is good enough to get on with. I feel very grey at present about the possibility of making a coherent system of the New Hebrides – or Malekula.

I have discovered perhaps 4 or 5 important new things, drum signalling, geometrical-figure drawing (amazingly intricate & ingenious), some secret societies with bull-roarer etc. a system of fertility-magic connected with sacred pottery & certain mythical culture-heroes; one or two interesting things about social organization.

But what seems to me more & more important is to try & construct some outline of the cultural history of the New Hebrides. Speiser tried to do something in that direction, in the field of material culture, in 1913. Rivers of course had an elaborate theory, still the best, but his work in Ambrym later (with Layard in Malekula) seems to me to raise very great objections to its acceptance. I have never seen however, any paper of Rivers' attempting to reconcile the two, or at least stating how far he considered his Ambrym work modified his 1908 expedition work. Then in 1922 or so Barnard suggested a scheme which, so far as I understood it from hurried reading of his thesis, was almost the exact reverse of Rivers'.

I believe if one could really make some decent historical analysis, a kind of stratification of the extraordinarily varied & complex cultures of the New Hebrides it might be possible, by relating this to (esp.) Papua & Mandated Territories cultures, to evolve (as Rivers did) a general scheme for W. Pacific cultures. To be sure of the analysis of one reasonably large area would be an incalculable aid; one could then set out on all kinds of ramifications. I must confess I don't share Malinowski's scorn (?) for the historical people. I realize more and more that I have only the vaguest idea of what is meant by 'sociology' and 'social psychology' – at least as practical sciences in which research is to be done. Oh Margou I would like to talk to you of a whole lot of difficult things – one of the most terrible things here is that you go living day after day with the same old impasses, never moving an inch further into or out of them, wondering in fact whether they really do exist or not. In London, or Cambridge, you can find out, you can get points settled, you can at least move a little way. Of course here one is perhaps, unwittingly, resolving something, but I am not entirely comforted by the reflection that something I do here may throw light on some more or less distant problem elsewhere. It is so different in physics & chemistry – there you have a vast structure of really beautiful theory, experimentally verified in enormous numbers of ways, and as undoubtedly true, I suppose, as anything of the kind one can think of – so research has a great theoretical searchlight, there is coherence and direction. Here (in ethnology) it is all a mess – I suspect most ethnologists are bad historians, or bad psychologists, or bad romanticists.

October

. . . I am sitting waiting, near the house, for some men who are coming to talk to me about offerings to ghosts etc. It is a most glorious, gorgeous day, a cool breeze coming in from the Pacific, all sparkling – gently swaying the palms: very very lovely. And marvellously soft and delicate scents – a kind of wild rose, a 'honey suckle', and some large red flowers – lilies? Many many trees are in blossom just now. The white branched erythrina, ringed with a scarlet carpet of its petals, the most beautiful perhaps of all. Unbearably unbearably dear, I want to be with you. The beauty of it is immeasurably more worth while than anything else; yes, than anything else; than anything I can do. If *only* it were immediate. To spend weeks and weeks booking passages and changing steamers, in clouds and clouds of irrelevant people – it's so appalling I almost believe it's a nightmare . . .

Here come the men and I must talk about offerings to ghosts. I am a ghost.

Bernard

I had told my parents that I meant to join Bernard in Sydney if he got the University lectureship. They were, as I had expected, outraged. 'Why, you're not even engaged,' said my mother. 'How do you know that he intends to marry you? How do you know that he won't just leave you high and dry?' This seemed to me utterly irrelevant: it had nothing to do with Bernard and me. However, I wrote and told him what they'd said, and got this characteristic answer:

Did I once say marriage was absurd? I do not really know much about it in England, even Europe. I do not think I would say it was absurd: I don't even remember saying it was absurd in general. I do not know how it stands in relation to us. In so far as it gives a sort of social status to sexual relations, it is perhaps necessary: I have no opinion in this matter, it seems essentially a matter for society or social opinion – whatever that may be – to decide . . . Since the beauty and the joy are by themselves, creating what they will, I cannot see that they have any relation to legal forms, which therefore depend on other grounds, social opinion, prudence, etc. – if they are necessary, I don't see it matters either way – impose them.

Bushman's Bay
N.E. Malekula
October 29th, 1926

Margou dear, I have moved across to the other side of the island for a short while. Why do French people use graph-paper for their correspondence? – I have just borrowed this from a Frenchman here. In this place it is more or less civilization, both a French and English steamer called, the latter is due tomorrow. I hoped to get a mail away by it. I need clothes badly – also a lot of tinned stuff. I don't know what to do about leaving or when to leave. There are so many things undone, unsolved & this is the last chance. I want to try and do some work on other islands, Ambrym & Oba, yet. And then overwhelmingly I want to be away, away especially from the whites here, back in Europe. But Haddon writes that there is little likelihood of any job of an anthropological nature going in England

& that an Australian will probably get the Sydney thing. I thought of applying for a Rockefeller grant or fellowship – Weinstein was working on one – but here I can get hold of no particulars. Haddon suggests vaguely that I might get another grant from Cambridge & wander off on another expedition, from Sydney – but that would be too terrible, tho' again I can see the overwhelming and urgent importance of it. My S.W. Bay notes to May have reached Cambridge, & Haddon says they're 'wonderful' – I confess it pleased me a little, somehow. It's absurd, because I think he's only gone through them quickly, and there are so many, so terribly many, gaps and faults and omissions, bitterly and acutely painful, that he has not seen: and I am ashamed, it is all too loathsome, horrible – I have never understood and always hated this team spirit and personal touch, it is so ugly, so irrelevant, marring things that are profoundly beautiful: and again and again I submit to it, and again and again I am bitterly ashamed.

A cutter has just come in, which is going up to Big Nambas territory on Monday. I am going to move up there, it is an extreme piece of luck, they are the only real 'cannibals' left – though not in the cinema sense of Martin Johnstone. (He filmed them a couple of years ago but the whole thing was a pack of lies – I think it was shown in London.)

My parents wanted me to go to Egypt with them in the New Year, so I wrote and asked Bernard what he wished me to do. He sent me a telegram saying 'Go Cairo. Letter follows.' That letter was written on December 9th, when he was again at Bushman's Bay. His mail had been very delayed and had only reached him a few days earlier. He was worried that he hadn't yet heard about the Sydney job and about the difficulties of making any plans at all.

If I get the Sydney job (which I think unlikely) you could come out at once. If I do not get it, I want to go on here for a little time yet. I have hit on what I think is something rather valuable in Ambrym – a class system of marriage of the type of those among the Central Australian aborigines – it clarifies the whole series of problems here, besides being, I think, of considerable importance in relation to Melanesian culture in general. I very very much want to follow it up as far as I can go. It is of course not in the direct track of my Malekulan work, but sufficiently valuable to make me leave the latter for a while and work it out. At present (for the last 3 weeks or so) I have been hung up by a sore developing from a swollen leg. I do not know what it is going to do. If it grows smaller and heals, I shall be able to get to work quickly, if not I may have to go to Noumea (New Caledonia) & get it better & then come back. It is rather a deep one, which makes it the more difficult to heal. In temperate climates they do not develop and heal quickly.

Margou, you ask for something definite. It is so difficult. I am overwhelmed by the sense that if I do not carry what I am trying to do to its completion, or rather, to its logical conclusion, to where I can be sure and inwardly calm and full of joy – I don't know how to describe it – it will leave me inwardly broken, there will not be my value to myself left. Since my work on Ambrym I am sure of myself at last, in a magical way. It is like a sudden illumination. So if I left now, I would know that I was sure and inwardly calm, but it would be cut off, unlived. If only I can go on, if only, and see further yet. I'm sorry, this all sounds so merely hysterical, and merely sensational, and it is not, it is calm and pure, purest joy, something pulsing and living again, as it was with you, as it will be with you . . . You see, it is really all the same thing and these great separating barriers of time and space make it falsely two things between which I must choose. It is intolerable, this inner oneness and this real, incessant conflict.

This Ambrym work has suddenly given me spiritual strength, but physically it has exhausted me. The physical exhaustion is nothing, but intolerably it makes more remote the time of breaking down these desert barriers and being completely with you, so all my activity is centred on being physically well – on being able to get this sore better above all.

Margou, now, what am I to plan if I do not get the Sydney thing? I can see only three things:–

1) I go on here, finishing perhaps in April, then home to England. It might be later, it depends so much on health and sickness.

2) You come out, say to Noumea, New Caledonia, by direct Messageries Maritimes from Marseilles, or other line. As I want to work some North New Caledonian native groups, we could go up there. There is no fever in New Caledonia, nor sores, one of the healthiest possible climates.

3) You wire for me, or write, and I come as soon as I can get things together and get away.

Of course I may get the Sydney job. In that case I would probably go straight there and come down here again in next summer vacation & finish things.

Margou dearest it is a burden like heavy pain to have to write you all this. Perhaps I am blind to you, perhaps it is all wrong, perhaps I am deceiving myself. Perhaps after all, all I am doing down here, all I have done, is muddy, crabbed shuffling about in ethnological puzzles. Good God!

I am very blind: I sometimes feel as if I were tapping about in the world with a stick, nearing and passing beautiful things and not seeing them. I am very blind about people.

Margou, if you want to come out and have the money, do please. And if you must be with me and can't come, wire to me, and I shall come.

Margou, I simply haven't the strength to leave now entirely of my own impulse. I feel bound. I'm sorry, so so sorry. And yet I want you so much to be with me.

Bushman's Bay
[Sometime in January 1927]

. . . I am just leaving for Ambrym with an old recruiting captain called Jeremiah Carmichael. It is Sunday, and very hot, a dead calm. There is sunlight in all the trees, brilliant tropical sun, very beautiful, and gay birds, martins & honey-eaters & cockatoos and the green and bronze pigeons, & large bright green lizards, and scarlet shrubs – amaranthus with crinkled tongues and acalypha, and purple, velvet-leaved coleus.

I have been reading *Evelyn Innes*, by George Moore. Somehow I feel the whole thing not worth while except for the actual writing, the prose is very beautiful. I feel that rather about all Moore's books that I've read – but I've only read two or three. I read a book by C. E. Montagu, too, called *Rough Justice*, and liked it.

Someday I want very much to go into the adjustments of plants & animals, parasites & hosts & so on: it fascinates me. I have been much stimulated, too, by Whitehead's book: thank you very much. I do not understand it yet. There seem to me to be a lot of difficulties in the theory of organic mechanism. So often he is rather loose and obscure: things like 'an underlying activity evolving in achievements of organism', 'enduring harmonies of shapes of value which merge into higher attainments of things beyond themselves'. Thus, taking the relation of electron & proton to atom & molecule, these to cells, unicellular & multicellular animals, organs & higher animals, reasoning & the 'realm of eternal objects' & logic, I am not clear in what way these are interdependent, as organisms within organisms. The chapter on the quantum theory is intensely interesting, he certainly seems to have succeeded, where no other physicists have done, in suggesting a way out. I wonder whether he has published the thing as a worked-out mathematical paper, in the *Philosophical Magazine* or elsewhere. I should like very much to discuss the book and the problems it seems to raise with someone like Broad. I do feel that it is most frightfully important just now to have as sound and complete as possible a philosophy of science. I have come more and more to feel that literature and the plastic arts have for me very little significance, especially compared with music: in that there is something beyond all things, so utterly the only meaning, the only beauty, the only truth, that all else seems an unbelievable nightmare: all good & loveliness seems to be in it & through it.

Bernard had spoken to me in Cambridge about his great love of music: it was almost a threat to him, he said, a complete world in which he could so easily have lost himself altogether. But I don't believe that he would ever really have shrugged off literature and the plastic arts: both – and particularly poetry – meant a very great deal to him.

The letter continued:

I shall be back as soon as I possibly can, Margou dear. Honest Injun. I have changed, I think, less than I thought, but it is difficult to say. You know what I could say to you, and how utterly apart from the depth and truth of things it is. Have I been wrong in all this, Margou dearest? Sometimes I have wretched thoughts, in this eternal waiting. Oh God, if only we could be together & know one another again. In this terrible barrier of time there is only a tangle & confusion. Only now it isn't so long, it is at least 1927 already.

In Cairo, on March 3rd, I got a telegram from Bernard saying 'Sydney lectureship begins April. Come.' My parents were indignant and trotted out all the old arguments, but I was determined to go.

The steamer on which Bernard had planned to leave Malekula was unusually late; perhaps if it had arrived on time he might have been saved. On March 5th he became feverish and two days later it was found that he had blackwater fever. The missionary couple in South West Bay nursed him as best they could, but in vain. He died on March 12th, not quite three months after his twenty-fourth birthday.

My uncle, to whom I had spoken about Bernard, read of his death in *The Times* and telegraphed my parents to break the news to me. I didn't know what to do. I just wanted to get away, somewhere, anywhere, away from Egypt, away from my parents, from everybody. I took the first boat I could back to England.

In London I found a letter from Bernard's mother. I hadn't known that he'd told her about me, but he had, and she had found out my address – from Dr Haddon, I suppose – and had written to share her grief with mine. We met: she was a delightful, very simple, very gentle woman, with a quiet sense of humour and utterly generous in her acceptance of me. Although we didn't meet often, we wrote to one another right up to the time of her death, more than thirty years later. When he had retired and come back to England, I also met Bernard's father, a man of most lively and far-ranging intellect, and he too wrote to me from time to time.

Bernard's last letter to me, written about three weeks before his death, only reached me more than a month after I was back in England. He had never written to me like that before, and I believe that in spite of the practical plans, in spite of the fact that a short time later he sent me the telegram to come, he really knew, deep inside himself, that it was a farewell letter. And the postscript, written across the top corner of the first page, seemed like a special message to make me want to go on living, a last reassuring wave of his hand before he left me for ever.

South West Bay
Malekula
Wednesday, February 16th

Margou dear, I'm at last packing up and leaving here – by the next boat, in about 10 days' time. Oh Margou dear, it has been so long, so long, so terribly long. After these intermiñable corridors of dreams there is still my body, but different, still the sensual world, but fainter, still the weary procession of thoughts, and yet this haunting, inescapable unreality. It has always been so; so seldom can I find myself. I know that *I* am not what I am now, what I am so much, just as I am not my body. This body and this mind are somehow simply views or constructions, from a sort of scientific standpoint, of certain levels, so ultimately unimportant in the thing, the total, the organism (??) that is I. And now I am shut and barred in by this mind and this body, and there is no means to seek the magic and the beauty and the fulfilment of that something which I still know somehow is the only truth, the only meaning of myself. So I write and think and act barrenly, like a man merely. How loathsome is this inescapable world of death. For it has nothing in itself but death. Only fools have thought otherwise.

Body has meaning in mind, but mind has meaning in something 'higher' (horrible word, weak, nauseating, blasphemous word). Margou dearest I am fond of you beyond all others, you I have loved face to face, not through a glass darkly in this world of death. I am fond of you beyond measure because you freed me from the world of death, and I knew you in the world of beauty and fulfilment. So I believe in you, because I remember you, even though I cannot know you now because I am in the world of death. So it is not I alone, nor you alone, but only being face to face.

I understand now the fearful fear of myself that has haunted me since – since as early as I can remember, since a child, till I fled anywhere, to the hot sun, to dragon flies and bees and snapdragons, to soldiers drilling and busy market-places, anywhere to forget the deathly meaningless horror of this body and this mind, ever present and pursuing, a shadow of something that I knew not. I came to realize, when I learnt what people called 'morbid', that this was 'morbid', but the reality of it was not diminished, probably it was increased by contemplating it. I see now, somehow, that this fear of the world of death is really the beginning of life, and that it is as inescapable in the market place at noon as alone in the night.

I am very tired, so my writing changes.

How I hate Cambridge: I liked my work there, particularly towards the end: its science is good. But for all else, what a terrible place.

How bitterly evanescent is the spirit, transient like the freshness of sun on flowers. That I might only know it more, so that I should have power to escape the world of death.

There is a marvellous poem by Verhaeren which I have tried long to remember, but cannot. He is profound and lovely beyond words, I have an intense desire and yearning for some of his stuff. The poem I am trying to remember belongs to his years of drifting and despair and night.

Margou dear, are you going to come to me? I have heard from Sydney that they've elected me lecturer in anthropology, I'm supposed to begin lecturing in April. I get only £400 or £450 a year (I forget which) with some annual increment of £40. As Radcliffe Brown says, it's very little. I've wired accepting the thing, since it's the only thing I can see at present. Brown writes that my work in Ambrym is 'one of the most important discoveries made in Melanesia' and so exciting that I should send a note about it to *Man* at once. It is just a new kind of class system regulating marriage. However, it is pleasant to be praised.

Lectures begin in the early part of April. Where I am to live in Sydney I don't yet know. In fact, I scarcely know anyone there.

Margou, I'm sorry for all the horrid mess things have been in. You see, I applied for the Sydney thing a long time ago, & had no reply for so long (owing to my mails going astray), that I did not know what to do. I didn't know whether the election had been made or not. I felt ill & wanted to go up to Sydney, yet I knew that if I did that there would be little chance of getting here again. As it is, I have, luckily, practically completed what I wanted to do here, & New Caledonia I hope to be able to tackle in one of the vacations – I believe, by the way, it is a lovely place. But you, Margou – what do you want? You see, I expect I shall only be able to finance myself and I know very little of what Australia, or Sydney, is like. dear, dear you, how long, how terribly long since I saw you and heard you and felt you. Till I have got fixed up in Sydney I can say

M.G. at Cambridge.

nothing about things, nothing definite I mean. What would you do in Sydney? Margou dear, all this arranging and scaffolding seems such meaningless dross: I want only to be together, together there might be such joy and beauty and fulfilment between us, we might know so much together. Place seems really immaterial. I wish all this had not to be written: dear, you understand. All I can say is that from April onwards I am in Sydney, getting about £33–35 a month. Do whatever you want, whatever you think best. I can conform to any scheme of morality. A half-caste is going to Noumea to have some operation on his throat, & will get this letter thru' to catch the French mail boat. I'll try & wire, but it is almost hopeless from here.

Bernard

P.S. Friday, early morning. It is a still, cool, cloudless morning. Off in a cutter to Lambumbu with this letter. There is peace and joy and calm everywhere, I feel well and indescribably happy.

Bernard

Epilogue

In the spring of 1982 I had a letter from Kirk Huffman, the curator of the Cultural Centre of Vanuatu – the name, since Independence in 1980, of the New Hebrides – telling me that the people of South West Bay in Malekula remembered Bernard Deacon, or remembered what their parents had told them about him, and that he had become for them almost a mythical, a cult figure. They believed that Bernard had had a 'special friend, a woman' and they had asked Kirk to find out whether I was still alive. If I was, they had said, they would like to see a photograph and to hear my voice.

Kirk and his beautiful and spirited Colombian wife, Claudia, came to see me when they were in England that summer and he took back with him a photograph and a recorded message. Later, when I had signed up for a tour in Australia, we decided that I should break off from it to stay with them in Vila, the capital of Vanuatu, and to visit Malekula.

I flew to Vanuatu from Sydney on the 5th of March, 1983. Vila, on the island of Efate, is a pleasant, leisurely, strung-out little town, hilly, full of blossoming trees and shrubs and with wonderful sudden glimpses of a silky-surfaced sea, brilliant blue, vivid green and a pale pinky mauve. The whole place, sauntering in the sun, seems utterly self-contained as though, despite its splashes of modernity – banks, little 'supermarkets', hotels, taxis, travel office and all the rest of it – it really has no truck with the outside world. Local politics, however, are absorbing and endlessly discussed.

Kirk dashed around everywhere, mercurial, off to see somebody else, to do something else, to telephone someone – and this could be quite a problem – always so very nearly unreliable and yet always producing the rabbit out of the hat at the last moment. It seemed that there was for ever something more that had to be said and he said it, top speed, in English, in French or in Bislama, the lingua franca of Vanuatu, a pidgin based on English and local

languages spiced with French. Eyes sparkling – 'Then whooshsh!'
he'd conclude some narrative, flinging out his right arm and
twirling his beard with his left hand. There was no stopping him:
whenever he wasn't speaking he was humming tunelessly beneath
his breath. I couldn't quite believe that he was running the
Cultural Centre so efficiently – but he was; I couldn't quite believe
that he would get me to Malekula – but he did.

We flew to Norsup, the airstrip at the northern end of Malekula
on March 11th. There's another airstrip in the making at South
West Bay and Kirk had hoped that we might go there on a trial
flight but, in my view luckily, there had been heavy rains and it
was waterlogged. So we went to Norsup and were met there by
Père Rodet, a Catholic missionary, a tall, thin man, cadaverous,
with a slight squint behind his severe glasses and a charming,
faintly malicious smile. I climbed up into the front of his Toyota
van, together with a young French school-teacher, while Kirk sat
in the open back with a couple of Malekulan men and the luggage.
We set off on the dirt road, built in 1979, narrow between
immensely tall coconut palms. Below were smaller trees and dense
green bushes with gigantic leaves, an impenetrable tangle.

Père Rodet stopped with a jerk at the sight of a group of small
boys and motioned them to climb into the back.

'Otherwise it would have taken them eight or nine hours,' the
school-teacher told me. 'That's what it used to take me before the
road was built. It wasn't so much the distance as the monotony.
Always the same, mile after mile.'

Père Rodet drove ferociously fast, down and up the switchback
precipices of the road and through the wide water splashes.

'What would happen if the truck broke down?' I asked.

He just looked at me and laughed.

At one point we passed a battered, rusty van lying on its side
some way below the road.

'Is the man still in it?' asked the school-teacher.

'Yes, we couldn't get him out,' said Père Rodet.

We drove for more than an hour before we came to Unmet, a
small hamlet – mission house, church, school and a few houses – in
an open space by the sea. Kirk and I were to stay in the mission
house and later in the evening Kirk was going to show a film of the
Big Nambas, for this was their territory. Père Rodet gave us tea

and then said, 'Come with me, I've something to show you,' and took us to the back of the house. Cut into the steep bank behind it was a cave with rough white coral sides.

'This is my *Nakamal* that I had built for the men to drink kava in the evenings. And those,' he said, pointing to a little stack of half coconut shells, 'are the drinking bowls. Of course I shouldn't have taken *you* in there at all,' he added with an amused look at me. 'Women are strictly forbidden to go inside.'

The film was projected on to the white wall of the schoolhouse, people from nearby villages sitting on the grass around. They were an orderly, rather quiet lot who broke into laughter and whispering when they spotted someone they recognised in the film. There were some splendid tribal dances but there was also the ritual killing of a pig by clubbing it to death while it struggled and squealed in loud and desperate protest. I hated that, but the audience laughed.

Later, when the men – Kirk, two French doctors and Père Rodet himself – had gone to drink kava, I was left with a young French woman vet.

'The film was interesting,' I said, 'but the killing of the pig was horrible.'

'It's the custom,' she said, 'You can't change it.'

'Even if you can't change it you can deplore it,' I said.

She gave me a contemptuous look, picked up a book and sat reading without another word. Père Rodet came back, exchanged a few remarks with her and then cleared the big table and set it for six people. And when the other three men returned we all sat down to a meal of fish stew, a big bowl of rice and a bottle of wine.

I had been in Malekula now for a few hours and I found it doubly strange. It was an utterly different world from any I had known before and it was also utterly different from that which Bernard had known. He had been told by the commissioner to stay in Big Nambas territory for only a very short time because of the danger: the Big Nambas were cannibals and hostile to white people. The men had worn nothing but a *nambas* – a penis wrapper and a bark belt: the women a fringe or a mat skirt and a mat head-dress. Today all the men wore shorts and loosely hanging shirts or T-shirts, while all the women wore the charming 'Mother Hubbards' – loose, flower-patterned cotton frocks, trimmed with lace and floating ribbons. What the Vanuatuans call 'custom dress' is certainly still worn in some bush villages in the interior and on ceremonial occasions, but round the coasts missionary clothes have prevailed. The orderly villagers watching Kirk's film-show seemed very remote from the cannibalistic Big Nambas of Bernard's day: this present Malekula had a solid, everyday existence; it was exotic but it was also just another place.

The boat to take us to South West Bay was due to arrive at eight o'clock next morning. At nine, when there was still no sign of it, Père Rodet said he would drive us to another beach where it might possibly have anchored. So off we set down the dirt road and after a mile or two turned abruptly into the bush – no road, not even a track – until we came to a standstill just beyond a little village of grass-roofed houses with walls of woven bamboo. We got out and walked uncomfortably through mud and tangled brushwood to the shore but still there was no sign of a boat.

'You'll never get to South West Bay,' remarked Père Rodet cheerfully.

At about half past ten, back in the mission house, there were shouts of *'Le bâteau arrive'* – but now, it seemed, there was after all no hurry.

'You'd better eat first,' said Père Rodet, and Kirk agreed. So we settled down to a leisurely meal of cans of beer and the remains of last night's supper. It was March the twelfth, a hot overcast day and the fifty-sixth anniversary of Bernard's death.

The boat was low in the water, bobbing restively from side to side below the jetty.

'Now!' said Kirk: the captain took my arm and between them they manoeuvred me aboard.

It was a small boat with a wooden canopy over two thirds of it under which our baggage was stowed behind the rusty diesel engine with its cracked funnel. All the paint was peeling or completely worn away; the one passenger seat was a rough and oil-stained plank laid across two petrol barrels and apt to tip up if you sat too near the end. The captain, bare legs dangling inside the boat, sat on the raised platform at the stern, the heavy wooden tiller in his hands and an abstracted look on his face. Behind him was an outrigger canoe that the crew had lashed on just before we started. The crew – there were two of them – spent most of the journey in the prow, hidden from me by the canopy, talking and smoking with Kirk. Every forty-five minutes or so they edged their way round to the open area where I was sitting, fiddled a bit with the engine, took up a floorboard and one of them, kneeling down, used a plastic quart jug to bale black, oily water into a bucket which the other emptied over the side.

'There's a leak, you see,' explained Kirk.

Once I tried to count the number of bucketfuls but it was a soporifically rhythmic performance and after about twenty I dozed off.

So we chugged along the coast of Malekula, the smelly heat of the engine mingling with the relentless heat of the day. I hadn't realised that the island was such a very large one: rounded hills, densely green, spilling right down to the sea with only an occasional cove edged with white sand to mark a possible landing place and, rarely, a straight, thin stem of smoke above the trees, indicating a village.

'It will take longer than a speed boat would,' Kirk had said, 'but it will be more comfortable.'

'How long will it take?' I'd asked.

'Oh, four or five hours,' he said.

Now he told me, 'We are going to stop at Vn'mavis. We had a message – there are some old men there who as children saw Bernard and they want to shake your hand.'

There was no jetty and the boat had to be anchored some distance from the shore. The villagers, fully dressed, waded out to us, a few carrying small children on their shoulders. I leant down over the side and shook their hands: some of the babies stretched theirs out to be shaken too but others stared at me in horror and started to bawl. The three old men stood hesitating on the strand till they were paddled out to us in an outrigger and hauled aboard. They sat in a row smiling at me and telling Kirk in Bislama how Bernard had passed through their village on his way to Lambumbu and had spent a night there.

It amazed me that there should still be such a vivid memory of Bernard who, after all, had been in Malekula for less than fifteen months more than half a century ago. In part, I think, it is due to the impression made by his rare personality, so very different from that of most of the other whites whom the natives had encountered.

Dr Haddon, in his preface to *Malekula* quotes a letter from Miss L. E. Cheesman, an entomologist who worked in Malekula in 1929 and 1930.

The natives who worked for him alluded to him with a nearer approach to affection than I have remarked in any Malekulan. I had at different times three of his boys as guides. At South West Bay I employed Amanrantus who is mentioned very often in Mr Deacon's notes. He described very graphically the surprise of bushmen when a white man visited them who learnt their language so that he was able to talk to them in it. Amanrantus accompanied him on most of his bush journeys, encamped with him, acted as interpreter, and waited on him during his last illness. He told me more than once how the bushmen liked Mr Deacon, who 'was good along boy belong island altogether' ('was good to all natives'). When passing the obscure grave among the coco-nuts I said that probably some day the friends of Mr Deacon would have a stone put up, Amanrantus begged to be allowed to do that work, repeating afterwards twice lest I had not understood that it was because it was for Mr Deacon.

Another of my guides, Tarlis, who took Mr Deacon coast journeys in his canoe (or else his brother did, I am not sure), mentioned that the natives were so surprised that he could make long treks on bush trails without fatigue. At Lambumbu I heard the same, and also how he would receive parties of natives, some of which came from long distances to visit him, and would patiently answer all their questions, show them pictures, and tell them about the world and especially of England. The natives there said of him 'Mr Deacon savvy too much all things altogether.' He must have made a deep impression on them, for they repeated to me things he had told them, giving me among others a very clear description of snow, which is of course a new idea to them. They also remembered all he had told them of his family, and were disappointed that I knew nothing about him.

And Mr E. Corlette, the planter in Bushman's Bay who had lived on the island for twenty-five years and whose house was the only one in Malekula in which Bernard had been able to enjoy both good talk and good books, wrote of him:

Amanrantus in middle age.

Sometimes I think they [the natives] thought he was a bit mad. They couldn't understand why he wanted the information and they could not exactly catalogue him. He could not be a missionary because he enquired into subjects that they knew were tabu to missionaries. He could not be a trader because he had nothing to sell, nor a recruiter because he didn't want them to work, nor anybody connected with the government because he didn't want to interfere with them in any way. Anyhow, I confidently believe he procured more insight into those things that were really valuable than any of his contemporaries or any who have tried previously.

As well as such personal recollections of Bernard which have been passed on to a new generation, it seems that his memory has been enshrined because of the recent great interest in 'custom' in Vanuatu, the desire to record its history and preserve its traditions. It is generally understood that Bernard made an important contribution to this and indeed I found that several people in South West Bay had read his book.

The boat chugged on and when, after five hours, we at last arrived opposite Wintua in South West Bay, we once more had to anchor some distance from the shore. At first it looked deserted but soon people appeared, running down from all directions – it seemed that they had waited for us on the strand for most of the afternoon but finally had given up and trickled home. The crew untied the outrigger and Kirk was the first to be paddled ashore and garlanded with a lei of white frangipani and scarlet hibiscus – not a Melanesian tradition but, as I was told rather apologetically later, the children had made the two garlands. When the canoe returned for me I was taken aback at the narrowness of the hollowed-out tree trunk and the spurious look of fragility – spurious because in fact, I'm told, outriggers are extremely stable. I was helped in, sat on the front cross-bar and rushed, with what seemed to me incredible speed, towards the shore. Then the canoe ground into the sand and, sandals in hand, I waded the last few yards to be greeted by Chief Kambong and garlanded. The whole chattering village escorted Kirk and me to the waiting Toyota truck and we were driven recklessly up the perilous few hundred yards to the mission house where we were to stay.

The three women who lived in the house – Enny, a Presbyterian deaconess, her young and very shy sister Mary and their friend Rosie – welcomed us into a large light room, simply furnished, with charming straw mats on the floor and jars of bright tropical flowers on the tables. A group of men followed us in: Chief Kambong Rantes and Elder Massing, Aïleh and Aïar Rantes, the two sons of Amanrantus who had so often been Bernard's guide and interpreter, and several others. Five or six small boys crept in too and squatted on the floor near the door. One of them started to point at each of us in turn and count us in English: the others took up the game, glancing at me mischievously to make sure that I was watching. The men were talking in Bislama, which of course I couldn't understand and which, it seemed, everyone in South West Bay spoke fluently as well as their own languages while most, even the children, could get along passably in English.

Soon the men went off to their kava drinking, the boys ran out and I had the luxury of a very hot bath: the water was solar heated. When I was dressed again, I found the table beautifully laid with dishes of taro, breadfruit, sweet potato and rice, some kind of fish, and coconuts with the top sliced off for drinking the milk.

'Come and have tea, Margaret,' said Enny.

'But what about Kirk?' I asked.

'Oh, you want to wait for him?' she said, her tone implying that this would be altogether wrong. I had yet to learn the extent to which men and women led separate lives.

'Oh no,' I said, and moved to the table.

When we had nearly finished eating, Chief Kambong came in and handed me a piece of paper.

'The programme for tomorrow,' he said.

The paper read:

Programme for Sunday 13th March 1983

1) After breakfast Magret will visit the Degon's grave at 8 o'clock.
2) After visiting the grave the Memorial Service will be held. During the Service offings will be taken. Speaches too.
3) After the Service every body will have dinner together in the honner of Magret.
During the Lunch the Presentation take place.

Monday 14th March

'The programme for Monday isn't decided yet,' said Chief Kambong. Enny said, 'Sit down and have something to eat,' which, after considerable hesitation, he did.

'I had heard,' I said, 'that there are stories about Bernard's spirit sometimes coming back to visit South West Bay.'

'What's that?' he asked sharply and I repeated it, though realising that I had made a mistake.

'Who said that? I never heard that,' he said angrily, and Enny, scowling, echoed, 'Never!' I quickly changed the subject.

Kirk had told me that on September 10th, 1980, he and a doctor from Pentecost, Edward Tambisari, had arrived by medical boat at Wintua, where all the chiefs of South West Bay were assembled. Kirk had shown them the film made by Martin Johnson and had then recorded an interview. They were all sitting in the clinic when Edward Tambisari ran in and asked who the white man was whom he had seen washing himself in the pool outside the village where Bernard used to wash. There was no white man – apart from Kirk – in the district and so they believed that it must have been Bernard's spirit that Edward had seen. They were frightened. After I had returned to Vila I had a long talk with Kaindum Baiagk Atis, a fieldworker for the Cultural Centre. He told me that in that same September, 1980, he and Kirk had walked up to Bernard's grave one evening and had sat on the hill and taken photographs. Kirk was staying with him in his house and they had both found it difficult to sleep. At about ten o'clock Kaindum woke, sure that there was someone in the house, shaking it. He couldn't see anybody but he was frightened and he wakened Kirk: he was convinced that it was Bernard's spirit, come to tell them that they must continue with his work. The next night the house was once more shaken. Kaindum also told me the story of the white man seen washing in the river pool at a time when there was no white man in the district.

When the Chief had left I moved to the little table on which stood a jam jar of flowers, and Mary, a lovely, slender girl of thirteen, sat herself down beside me.

'Those are beautiful flowers,' I said.

'I pick them,' she said. 'I pick all the flowers in this room.'

She looked at me intently and then began to laugh, covering her face with her hands in embarrassment.

'Why do you laugh at me?' I asked.

'I don't laugh at you,' she said. 'I think you good.'

There was a bellowing and the sound of raised voices outside and Mary ran to the door to see what was happening.

'What was that about?' I asked when she came back.

'She want to kill a cow,' she explained in her gentle voice and smiling.

Graves have no meaning for me, no connection with the reality of the buried person. I didn't want to visit Bernard's grave but I knew that it was expected of me, indeed that it was considered to be the main object of my coming to Malekula and that the villagers would be affronted if I didn't go. So at nine o'clock next morning – inevitably an hour late – I climbed once more into the Toyota and Chief Kambong put a jar of very beautiful flowers into my hands.

'For the grave,' he said, and I was touched by his thoughtfulness. It seemed that the whole village was coming with us, walking alongside the truck with a troop of excited children running ahead. We drove up a very steep track that looked little used, with newly slashed bushes on either side.

'I do hope I can go alone,' I said rather desperately to Kirk. He nodded and spoke to the Chief who, when we came to a fence, told the people to hold back and gestured to me to go through the gate and further up the hill.

It was rough going, and when I came to a little burial ground I stumbled around, clasping my jar of flowers, unable to find the right grave. I looked back in dismay at all the watching people by the fence: the Chief ran forward, signing to me to go on further up. At the very top of the hill I found Bernard's grave with, a little further down, that of the Presbyterian missionary's wife, Mary Boyd, who died a few months after him.

Bernard's headstone was a plain rectangular slab with the words 'A. B. Deacon Anthropologist 1903–1927' engraved upon it. Now it was surrounded by jars and tins of flowers and hung with little garlands – moving tributes from the villagers for this special occasion. I added my jar and turning, looked down the hill on the

A dance performed in honour of M.G's visit to South West Bay.
(Photograph by Kirk Huffman)

other side where, through the trees, there was a glimpse of the sea. Suddenly, for some inexplicable reason and despite my belief that graves are irrelevant, I was glad that Bernard had been buried within sight of the sea.

I walked slowly back down the hill and was grateful to Kirk when he quietly took my arm and helped me up into the Toyota. It was only after my return to England that I discovered that although Bernard's mother had arranged with a missionary, a Mr Frayter, for a memorial for Bernard to be made out of a native wood – teak or mahogany – and to be carved by Amanrantus, when the French anthropologist, Jean Guiart, visited Malekula in 1950 he found Bernard's grave only earth covered and unmarked. Professor Guiart wrote to me:

> Finding the tomb in the bush without the coloured shrubs they always put on tombs, I asked the pastor of the village if they would build a cement tombstone if I gave them the money. The pastor came back the next day saying they would take my money for buying the cement but they would do the work free as they remembered Bernard as a good man to them in the time when they badly needed friends . . . I came back a few months later. The work had been done and everything was in order.

The memorial service was held in a big, barnlike, grass-roofed open-sided structure. I was made to sit on the platform with the chiefs and elders and with Kirk beside me to translate the long, long speeches in Bislama, interspersed with hymn singing. The congregation was mostly women and children but when the choir was announced a group of men, who had been lurking behind the building out of sight, filed in and sang. The sermon was preached at inordinate length and with many oratorical repetitions by Pastor Alec Luwan. It contained much praise of Mr Boyd, the missionary in whose house Bernard had stayed in South West Bay, unhappily enduring his denigration of anthropology and anthropologists. It was as if Pastor Luwan were claiming Bernard in support of the interests of the Church as against those of 'custom' although, in his account of the reasons for Bernard's death, he invoked tribal magic. Only very old people, Malekulans believe, die natural deaths: all others die because they have flouted 'custom', violated tabus. Pastor

Luwan said that Bernard had wanted to visit Melpmes, the most sacred of all the villages in the district and one that other villagers only approached with fear. Twice Bernard had asked for permission to go there and twice he had been answered 'No!'. Finally he went without permission and took photographs of some sacred objects and it was because of this, the Pastor said, that he had died.

At long last the sermon ended and I went back to the mission house to rest until the dinner was ready. When I returned I found that the entire edge of the barn had been lined with enormous leaves – I think they were banana leaves – upon which had been set little heaps of meat garlanded with taro and breadfruit cakes, one heap for each member of the congregation, already squatting beside it. I was honoured with a knife and fork: everybody else ate with their hands.

After the dinner came the presentations. My present to South West Bay was a book of photographs of Bernard as a boy and at Cambridge, enlarged from snapshots that his mother had given me: their present to me was a straw object which Annie, a small grey-haired woman who, as a girl, had been a servant in the Boyds' house when Bernard died there, handed to me shyly and without a word.

'What is it?' I asked, puzzled. 'A fly whisk?'

'No, it's a grass skirt,' said Kirk.

So I unrolled it and pretended to put it on, which caused considerable amusement.

While Kirk was helping me to roll it up again in the correct fashion, Chief Kambong held out an envelope.

'For me?' I asked, uncertain. He nodded.

When I opened it I found that it was stuffed with notes, the entire takings of the collection. 'Oh, but I can't accept money,' I cried in consternation and without thinking. The chiefs looked distressed and started to consult among themselves.

'Take it,' advised Kirk. 'Just take it.'

To avoid giving offence I thanked them warmly for their generosity and took it.

Chief Kambong then announced, on behalf of all the chiefs of South West Bay, the programme for the next day. 'At one o'clock,' he said, 'dancing! So that Mrs Margaret can see some of the things that Deacon saw when he was here. She has come all this long way to visit us and now we think of her as our mother and our sister. So everybody must come tomorrow – everybody. And there will be a football match as well,' he added.

More than three hundred people had partaken of the dinner and as they filed out I had to shake hands with every single one. Some of the women were too shy even to look at me and walked past with outstretched hand and averted head. One little boy slipped a pebble into my hand with a conspiratorial look – but whether it was meant as a present or as a joke I'm not sure.

Next morning Enny walked with me to the nearby village of Lorlow, passing the river pool where Bernard used to wash and where women now stood washing clothes, banging them on flat rocks, chattering and calling out to each other and to us. The village looked to me as though it had been built without plan, haphazard, as though a handful of houses had been tossed up to take root and grow wherever they happened to fall. Enny pointed to a larger roof just visible behind a fence of leafy saplings.

'That's the men's house,' she said.

'Have you ever been inside it?' I asked.

She laughed at my ignorance. 'Oh, no,' she said. 'Women don't go into it.'

One o'clock came and nothing at all seemed to be happening. However, about an hour later a couple of men carrying a slit drum – a hollowed out tree trunk – walked slowly on to the big field opposite the mission house and set it down on the grass. Gradually more drums were brought – eight or nine of them – and laid down to form a roughly oval-shaped cluster. Then several young men sat astride them and gave a short preliminary burst of drumming to summon people from outlying villages, while those from Wintua itself were drifting in, standing in little groups or lining up against the field fence. I was brought a chair and another was fetched for a tall grey-haired Chief who sat himself beside me. A very small boy toddled up to him and lolled against his knees, staring at me intently and holding out his hand to me. When I held out mine towards him, he slapped it with a look of delighted triumph.

'My niece's son,' the Chief explained: there seemed to be an easy understanding between the two of them.

Now the drumming began in earnest and a group of men moved into the field, bare breasted, wearing headbands stuck with feathers or bunches of leaves and carrying spears or long, old-fashioned muskets. Two or three of those from bush villages wore nothing but *nambas* with a flourish of leafy twigs tucked into the belt at the back. One small white-haired old man held a tall pole with a crest of leaves upright in one hand while with the other he held that of his neighbour.

'He's blind,' the Chief told me.

Singing a monotonous song, the men circled round and round the drums with small almost hesitant steps in time with the drumming, while at the edge of the field two grey-haired women – presently joined by a third – took similar little steps, backwards and forwards, backwards and forwards, throughout the long performance.

'That's how our women dance,' said the Chief. But none of the younger women joined in: they were standing in little groups, holding babies and chattering together, men wandered here and there in the increasing crowd, a small boy abstractedly tapped the fence in rhythm with the drums, and the dancers, utterly intent, moved round and round, singing their monotonous song. Casualness and ceremony were strangely intermingled.

At last the drumming stopped, the dancers left the field and I thought that the show was over. But suddenly the drums crashed out again and a second troop of men came dancing in, their bodies splodged with yellow ochre and wearing magnificent great helmet masks, painted black, white and red, anklets of clustered nuts that jangled as they moved, and with leafy branches sprouting from their belts. The drumming grew more and more urgent until, with a furious flourish, it ended abruptly only to start again in a few moments and work up once more to a sudden climax and a sudden ending – a pattern that was repeated over and over again while, in the background, the football match had already started. It went on long after the dancers had gone and the drums had been carried away.

'Where did those marvellous masks come from?' I asked Enny.

'I expect that they had been stored in the men's house in Lorlow,' she said.

'Yes, but who made them? What are they made of?' I asked. Enny smiled at the absurd innocence of my question.

'I think you'd better ask the men,' she said.

Later, back in the mission house, Kirk announced, 'We've all been invited to supper with Amanrantus' sons.'

It was after dark when the two men arrived to fetch us, lighting the way with electric torches through little lanes between grass-roofed houses with woven bamboo walls.

'Here we are,' said Aïleh. Bending our heads we went through the low doorway into the house, a single large, rectangular room lit by hurricane lamps and with no furniture apart from a table and several chairs near the door. The two wives and the sister of the Rantus brothers were spreading mats on the floor when we arrived: in the middle of the room there was a low circular mound covered with banana leaves and in the far corner there was a little pit beside which lay a bundle of sticks and a scatter of round stones.

Having installed us, the men went off to their kava drinking and I was left with the women and a growing number of small children running around and crawling about the floor, coming closer and closer to inspect me and daring me with little games of proffering things and then snatching them back. Meanwhile Enny explained the cooking arrangements: the sticks would be ignited in the little pit and the stones piled on top of them. When the fire had burnt out the stones would be transferred to the centre of the room and covered with leaves upon which the food would be placed. This in turn would be covered with leaves and in that 'oven' the food would cook until it was time to eat.

When the men returned we all squatted round the oven, whipped off the top leaves and there lay a whole little pig surrounded by taro, breadfruit and sweet potato cakes. The children darted in, snatched out titbits and ran off to devour them while the rest of us put our hands in and ate more soberly. It was a splendid offering, a real feast, and I felt ashamed of my squeamishness over the pig, the so very naked, complete little pig.

As we were leaving, Aïleh Rantes, Amanrantus' elder son, came up to me and handed me a photograph.

'I want to give you this,' he said. 'It is my father, Amanrantus, Mr Deacon's friend.'

We had to leave next morning. A party came down to the beach to see us off and there was much handshaking. Enny gave me a basket, Rosie a fly whisk and Mary a hand-carved wooden comb and I gave them brightly coloured scarves.

M.G. with some children in Aileh's house in Wintua, 1983.
(Photograph by Kirk Huffman)

'You know who I am?' asked Chief Kambong, still holding my hand and looking me full in the face, as though he doubted it.

'Why, yes,' I said.

'I am Chief Kambong,' he said.

'I know, Chief,' I answered, and we shook hands again. And once again I climbed into the outrigger and was paddled out to the boat.

In Vila, before I left Vanuatu, I had a long talk with Kaindum Baragh Atis, a Malekulan and a fieldworker for the Vanuatu Cultural Centre. His father was the old blind man I had seen led by the hand in the dance and his mother came from Melpmes, the sacred village where some say Noah's Ark is kept.

'Melpmes,' Kaindum said, 'is the most important village, the source of many things. People are scared to visit it.' And Kaindum repeated Pastor Luwan's tale of how Bernard had twice been refused permission to go there and how he had finally gone without permission, had taken photographs of a sacred ritual and that same evening on his return had fallen sick of the illness from which he died. Kaindum added that his father had told him how a number of Wintua people had accompanied Bernard on his way to Melpmes but had stopped outside the village, frightened to go further. But one old man sang out, as Bernard went on alone, 'Your food is coming!'

'Why do you imagine that his visit and his illness were connected?' I asked.

'Poison, perhaps,' said Kaindum.

'How could it have been poison? He was ill for five days before he died.'

'Some poisons work quickly and some slowly,' Kaindum said. 'And there was no need to make him eat or drink anything. A poisoned arrow pointed at him would have been enough.'

In August 1926 Bernard had written to Dr Haddon, 'Incidentally, actual poisoning in one sense of the word is very frequently practised with fatal results by the natives who, of course, class it with "magical" poisoning without differentiation & therefore no action is taken by the Govt.'

'Well,' said Kaindum. 'How do *you* think he died?'

'Of blackwater fever,' I said.

[75]

Kaindum looked at me and shook his head. And then he repeated the story that had been told to Kirk in an interview with Jack Maemae Sua on September 11th, 1980 and which Kirk has translated for me from Bislama.

'I just want to say a few words about the time Deacon came to study "Kastom". When he became sick, Mrs Boyd and Missionary Mr Boyd looked after him. When he realised that he was going to die he told the Boyds, "If I die put me in the grave with my feet facing north and my head facing south." This means that he came to study "kastom", died, but as his feet face north towards Melpmes his work will not die but go ahead. His work cannot die.'

'What do *you* think it means?' I asked Kaindum.

'It means that Deacon left his footprints on Malekula and these will remain. His work cannot die.'

D1095748

THE STORIES OF
THE MONTHS AND DAYS

THE RETURN OF PERSEPHONE

From the painting by Lord Leighton, P.R.A. By permission of the
Committee of the Leeds City Art Gallery

[*Page 75*

THE STORIES

OF THE

MONTHS AND DAYS

BY

REGINALD C. COUZENS

*With Illustrations from
Famous Paintings and Statuary*

DETROIT
Gale Research Company • Book Tower
1970

This is a facsimile reprint of the
1923 edition published in New York
by Frederick A. Stokes Company.

Library of Congress Catalog Card Number 70-124662

Contents

Contents

Illustrations

THE STORIES OF THE MONTHS AND DAYS

INTRODUCTION

Our Divisions of Time

How familiar to us are the names of the months, and the days of the week, and yet how few of us know to whom we owe these names or what a wealth of meaning they possess. They have come to us from the past, from the time when people worshipped many gods and explained the wonders of nature in their own simple way. But before listening to the stories which these names can tell us, we ought first of all to remind ourselves of the way in which our divisions of time came into being.

We all know that the earth turns round on its own axis, giving us periods of light and darkness, which we call day and night. The word "day", which comes from a very, very old word meaning "to shine", really means, of course, the time during which the earth is lit up by the sun, but it has also come to mean the time which the earth takes to revolve, as from sunrise to sunrise, sunset to sunset, midday to midday. The Greeks measured the day from sunset to sunset, the Romans from midnight to midnight, the Babylonians from sunrise to sunrise. The day, in this sense, became the first measurement of time.

The day, however, is a very short period, so another measurement was taken for a longer space of time, and this measurement was suggested by the changes in the moon. It was noticed that the moon altered in shape, beginning with the new moon, waxing to the full moon, and then gradually waning. So the space of time from one new moon to the next—about $29\frac{1}{2}$ days—was called a *moonth* or *month*, afterwards known as the lunar month (lunar, from Latin; *luna* = moon).

The next measurement of time, the year, was suggested by the seasons. People noticed that there was a period of heat and a period of cold, a time when the trees and plants put forth their buds, and a time when all Nature seemed to die, and these periods became known as the Seasons —Spring, the time when plants spring up; Summer, the mild or gentle season; Autumn, the season of increase, when the fruits of the earth are gathered in; Winter, the windy or cold season.

It was found that the time from one Spring to the next, or from one Winter to the next, was about twelve lunar months, and these twelve months were known as a year. The change of season is, of course, due to the movement of the earth round the sun, and the exact time taken by the earth is 365 days, 5 hours, 49 minutes. Now, a year of twelve lunar months is only 354 days, and the result of this difference was that the months got ahead of the seasons, and in a year or two, when, according to the Calendar, the Spring months had come, it was really still Winter. In order to put this right, the lunar year (moon year) was made longer by having an extra month put in every now and then. In this way the lunar year was made to correspond more nearly to the solar year (sun year), that is, the year of $365\frac{1}{4}$ days. The Jews put in a month seven times in every nineteen years, and the Greeks a month three times in every eight years.

The Romans had first of all a year of only ten months, beginning with March. Then they added two months, making a year of 355 days.

But even now the number of days was short, and to make up for the loss, days were added from time to time. These extra days, however, were added in such a way that they led to great confusion, and the Roman Dictator, Julius Cæsar, in order to do away with this confusion, decreed that the year 46 B.C. should consist of 445 days, and fixed the length of future years at 365 days. But since the earth's journey takes 365 days, 5 hours, 49 minutes, a quarter of a day was still lost each year, so Cæsar ordered an extra day to be put on to February every fourth year, making that year what we call Leap Year, because the Calendar makes a "leap" of one day. This new Calendar is called the Julian Calendar, after Julius Cæsar.

The lunar year, that is, the year of twelve months, seemed at last to be of the right length, but even now there was a very tiny mistake. You will have noticed that 5 hours, 49 minutes was taken as a quarter of a day, but it is short of 6 hours by 11 minutes. A very small difference you will say; but after several hundred years it amounted to ten days, so that the lunar year was now too long. In 1582 Pope Gregory ordered that ten days should be left out in that year, and the day after the 4th of October was called the 15th.

The change was not made in England until 1751, when eleven days were dropped, and it led to a great deal of discontent among uneducated people, who thought that these days had been stolen from them! In order to prevent the mistake occurring again, it was arranged that instead of every fourth year being a leap year, the years which end in 00, as 1700, 1800, 1900, should not be leap years.

CHAPTER I

January—The Month of Janus

The first month was called Januarius by the Romans, after Janus, the god of doors and gates. We see the same word in *janua*, the Latin for a gate or opening. From the idea that a door is a way in, an entrance, it became a custom among the Romans to pray to Janus whenever they undertook a new work. He was also the god of the beginning of the day, and it was only natural that when a new month was added at the beginning of the year it should be named after him. During this month offerings to the god were made of meal, frankincense, and wine, each of which had to be quite new.

Since a gate opens both ways, Janus was thought to be able to see back into the past, and forward into the future, and he was usually represented in pictures as having a double head that looked both ways. On the earliest Roman coins he is drawn with two bearded faces, with a staff in one hand, and a key in the other. He was also the protector of trade and shipping, and on some coins his head is shown with the prow of a ship. When people wished to picture him as the god of the year, they drew him holding the number 300 in one hand, and 65 in the other.

Janus was worshipped on the Janiculum (Hill of Janus), one of the seven hills on which Rome was built. Since he was the God of Gates, all the gates of Rome were under his care, especially the archway through which the army marched to war, and by which it returned. This archway was afterwards replaced by a temple which was called Janus Quadrifrons—that is, four-sided— because it was square. On each side of the building there were three windows and one door, making twelve windows and four doors, which represented the twelve months and the four seasons. In times of war the temple gates were kept wide open since people were continually making offerings to the god, but whenever there came a time of peace, the gates were at once closed. As we know the Romans were continually fighting, it does not surprise us to find that the gates of the temple were closed only *three times* in seven hundred years.

Janus was said to be the son of Apollo, the God of the Sun, whose daily task it was to drive across the sky in his chariot of fire. Each morning when Aurora, the Goddess of the Dawn, had opened the gates of the East, Apollo set forth, and when, his task accomplished, he reached the Western Ocean, he returned to his palace in the East.

> "And the gilded car of day
> His glowing axle doth allay
> In the steep Atlantic stream:
> And the slope sun his upward beam
> Shoots against the dusky pole,
> Pacing toward the other goal
> Of his chamber in the East."
>
> MILTON—*Comus.*

Apollo had another son, named Phæton, who one day persuaded his father to allow him to drive the sun chariot. All went well for a time, and then Phæton, being a reckless boy, began to drive too fast. He soon lost control of the horses, which plunged madly along and bore the chariot far from its track. It went so close to the earth that the fields were scorched, the rivers were dried up, and even the people were turned black—and they are black to this day! The

AURORA BEFORE THE CHARIOT OF THE GOD OF THE SUN

From the painting by Guido Reni in the Rospigliosi Palace, Rome

Here the goddess of dawn is shown scattering flowers before the car of day, which is surrounded by the dancing Hours.

[*Page 16*

cries of the terrified people attracted the attention of Jupiter, the king of the gods, who became enraged when he caught sight of the daring boy in the chariot of the sun. Taking up one of his thunderbolts, he hurled it at Phæton, who, scorched by its fire, fell headlong to the earth.

Another sad story told of Apollo is that of his friendship with a youth named Hyacinthus, to talk with whom Apollo used often to come down to the earth. Zephyrus, the God of the South Wind, was very fond of Hyacinthus too, and one day as Apollo and Hyacinthus were playing a game of quoits, Zephyrus came by. Filled with jealousy at the sight of Apollo and his friend, he blew Apollo's quoit aside so that it struck Hyacinthus and killed him. Apollo was greatly distressed at his friend's death, and in order that he might never be forgotten, changed the fallen blood-drops into clusters of flowers, which we still call Hyacinths.

> "For so Apollo, with unweeting hand,
>   Whilom did slay his dearly loved mate,
>   Young Hyacinth born on Eurotas' strand,
>   Young Hyacinth the pride of Spartanland,
>   But then transformed him to a purple flower."
>
> MILTON.

Another flower which should always remind us of Apollo is the sunflower. A story says that there once lived a girl named Clytie, and that each day, with eyes full of love for the fair sun god, she watched him journey across the sky: but Apollo, knowing nothing of her love, took no heed of her as he passed. Clytie watched for him day after day on a river bank, and her heart sank as each evening she saw his chariot dip down into the West. She would not leave the river bank, but stayed all through the cold night, anxiously waiting for the first flash of the sun's rays from the glowing East. At last the gods took pity on her, and changed her into a sunflower. Her green dress became green leaves, and her golden hair became yellow petals. Now was she happy indeed, for she knew that she could always see Apollo, and you will find that to this day the sunflower turns its head towards the sun as it moves across the sky.

Aurora, the Goddess of the Dawn, whom we have mentioned as opening the gates of the East for the sun god Apollo, married a mortal, Tithonus, a prince of Troy. In order that their happiness might know no end, Aurora begged Jupiter to grant Tithonus immortality. The wish was granted, but in her anxiety that Tithonus should never be taken from her by death, Aurora forgot to ask also for the gift of eternal youth. As the years went on Tithonus grew old and weak and became only a burden to her. At length, tired of his shrill voice and constant complaints, she turned him into a grasshopper, whose shrill complaining note is known to all.

The name for this month among the Angles and Saxons was Wulfmonath (Wolf month), since it was the time of year when the wolves were unable to find food, and their hunger made them bold enough to come into the villages.

CHAPTER II

February—The Month of Purification

This month did not always hold its present position, but was originally the last month in the year. The name is taken from a Latin word, *februare*, meaning "to make pure".

In the Palatine Hill, another of the seven hills of Rome, was a cave dug in the rock, and in it stood an image of the god Lupercus covered with a goat's skin. Lupercus was the God of Fertility or springing into life, and on the 15th of February a great festival was held in his honour. Sacrifices of goats and dogs were made; then the priests cut up the skins of the goats, twisted the pieces into thongs, and ran through the city striking all who came in their way. As in the very earliest times it was the shepherds who held this festival, it is thought that this running about with thongs meant the purifying of the land. The idea of the whole festival seems to have been one of purifying, of a new life, so the name chosen for the month in which it was held was one formed from a word meaning "to make pure".

There are some who think that Lupercus was the same as Pan, the God of the Shepherds. Pan was said to have been a son of Mercury, but he was not like the other gods; his body was covered with goat's hair, and his feet and ears were also like those of a goat. He was very fond of music and dancing, and spent most of his time in the forests playing with the wood nymphs—beautiful girls who lived among the trees. One day he saw a wood nymph, named Syrinx, with whom he fell in love, but she was frightened and ran away from him, and when Pan pursued her she prayed to the gods for help. She was at once changed into a clump of reeds, and Pan, in his disappointment, broke off seven pieces of the reed, bound them together, and so made an instrument of music, which was called the Syrinx after the beautiful wood nymph.

The invention of the Syrinx by Pan has been

wonderfully described by Elizabeth Barrett Browning in a poem which begins:

> " What was he doing, the great god Pan,
>   Down in the reeds by the river?
>   Spreading ruin and scattering ban,
>   Splashing and paddling with hoofs of a goat
>   And breaking the golden lilies afloat
>   With the dragon-fly on the river."

This story of Pan and Syrinx reminds us that the Greeks and the Romans imagined the mountains, the valleys, the woods, and the rivers to be peopled with lesser gods and goddesses, whose task of caring for the trees, the flowers, and the grass was appointed them by Jupiter. The woodland gods were known as Satyrs, and like their leader, Pan, were half man and half goat. Another famous satyr was Silenus, who was put in charge of Bacchus, one of Jupiter's sons, and the God of Wine. Silenus taught Bacchus, and accompanied him on his travels on the earth. The God of Wine rode in a chariot drawn by wild beasts, Silenus following him on an ass, and with them a merry company of nymphs and satyrs crowned with ivy leaves, who danced and sang and made music in praise of Bacchus.

" And as I sat, over the light blue hills
  There came a noise of revellers; the rills
  Into the wide stream came of purple hue—
    'T was Bacchus and his crew!
  The earnest trumpet spake, and silver thrills
  From kissing cymbals made a merry din—
    'T was Bacchus and his kin!
  Within his car, aloft, young Bacchus stood
  Trifling his ivy-dart, in dancing mood,
      With sidelong laughing."

KEATS—*Endymion.*

Many stories are told of the wood nymphs,
as the Goddesses of the Woods were called.   One
of the most famous is that of the nymph Echo,
who fell deeply in love with the beautiful Narcissus, whom she met hunting in the forest.
Narcissus, however, took but little notice of her,
and Echo's love soon turned to hatred and anger.
She prayed to Venus, the Goddess of Love,
that Narcissus might be punished for his hard-
heartedness, and then sorrowfully hiding herself
among the mountains, pined away until only her
voice remained, and in lonely places the voice
of Echo still answers those who call.

Meanwhile Venus sought an opportunity for
punishing Narcissus by making him suffer in the
same way as Echo had done.   One day Narcissus,

hot and thirsty with hunting, came to a shaded pool, and, as he stooped to drink, saw in the clear water the face, as he thought, of a water nymph. So beautiful was she that Narcissus was filled with love for her, and eagerly stretched out his arms; but no sooner did his hands touch the water than she vanished. He drew back in surprise and waited anxiously till the ruffled water became smooth, when again he saw the beautiful nymph. He spoke to her, and her lips answered him, though he heard no sound; he slowly put out his hands towards her, and her hands came to meet his. Sure now of her love, he tried a second time to clasp her in his arms, but, as before, she vanished. Again and again he strove to seize the nymph, but each time she escaped his grasp. Amazed, Narcissus sank down by the pool and gazed upon that lovely face, which seemed to mock him, and yet held him there. Apollo and his chariot sank into the Western sea, but the Goddess of the Moon shone on the water and showed the nymph still answering his words and holding out her arms to him. The days passed, and Narcissus, unable to tear himself away, grew pale and weak, watching the face, which also grew pale with despairing love.

Thus was Echo avenged, for Narcissus slowly starved himself to death through love for his own image! The gods, however, took pity on him and changed his body into a cluster of flowers, which have ever since borne his name.

We have associated Pan, the God of the Shepherds, with this month, and his name is found in a very familiar word in our language. He took a great delight in frightening travellers by creeping up behind them in the dark, and the fear with which he filled them was called "panic".

It is interesting to note that just as the Romans held a ceremony of purification during the month of February, so the Christian Church holds the feast of the Purification of the Virgin Mary on the second day of the month. The feast is called by Roman Catholics, Candlemas, because it is the custom to have a procession in which candles are carried, and it is on this occasion that the candles to be used in the church during the year are consecrated.

The weather at Candlemas is said to show what the weather will be like during the year, and an old proverb says:

> " If Candlemas is fair and clear,
> There 'll be twa winters in the year ".

CHAPTER III

March—The Month of Mars

This month, originally the first in the year, is named after Mars, the God of War. He was the son of Jupiter and Juno, the king and queen of the gods, and was generally represented in a shining suit of armour, with a plumed helmet on his head, a spear in one hand, and a shield in the other. His chariot was driven by the Goddess of War, Bellona, who also watched over his safety in battle; for the gods often took part in the battles which were constantly raging on the earth. During the great fight between the gods and the giants to decide who was to rule the world, Mars was captured by two of the giants, who bound him with iron chains and kept watch over him day and night. After over a year of captivity he was freed by the clever god Mercury, who succeeded in loosening the chains so silently that the giants heard no sound. Mars also took part in the Trojan War, when he was actually wounded.

Mars was loved by Venus, the Goddess of Beauty, but wishing to keep their love a secret from the other gods, they met only during the night, and Mars appointed his servant Alectryon to keep watch and to call him before the sun rose, as he did not wish Apollo, the Sun God, to see them. One night Alectryon fell asleep, and so was too late to warn Mars of the sun's approach. Apollo saw them from his chariot as he drove across the sky, and told Vulcan, the God of Fire, who caught them in a net of steel, and thus held them prisoner, while the other gods made fun of them. As soon as he was set free, Mars, who was filled with anger against Alectryon for failing in his duty, changed him into a cock, and driving him into a farmyard, condemned him to give warning every day of the sun's rising—a fanciful explanation why

> " the cock with lively din,
> Scatters the rear of darkness thin".
>
> MILTON—L'Allegro.

The gods, though they themselves were immortal—that is, could never die, nor even

grow old—yet sometimes married mortals, the
men or women whom they found on the earth,
and Mars fell in love with a beautiful girl named
Ilia, who had given up her life to serve in the
temple of Vesta, the Goddess of Fire. It was
the duty of these priestesses of Vesta to guard
the fire which continually burned on the altar of
the goddess, for the safety of the people was
thought to depend on this sacred flame. No
Vestal, as these priestesses were called, was
allowed to marry, under penalty of death. Ilia,
however, in spite of her solemn promise, consented to marry Mars, and keeping her marriage
a secret, continued to live in the temple. In
course of time she had two sons, Romulus and
Remus. Her father and mother, hearing that
she had broken her vow, ordered the full punishment of her crime to be carried out; the mother
was buried alive, and the children were left in
the forest to be killed by the wild beasts.

Thus Ilia perished, but the children were
wonderfully saved, so the story tells us, by a
wolf, who cared for them as if they had been
her own young. They were soon after found by
a shepherd, who took them to his home, where
they grew up to be strong and brave men. As

soon as they had reached manhood they left their home and went out into the world to seek their fortune. Coming to a beautiful country of hills and valleys, they decided to build a great city; but before they had even finished the outer walls, they quarrelled about the name which was to be given to it when it was built. Romulus lost his temper and struck his brother Remus, so that he fell dead to the ground. With the help of a band of wicked and cruel men like himself, Romulus at last succeeded in building a city, which, called Rome, after its founder's name, was to become one of the most famous cities the world has ever known.

Romulus became the first king of Rome, but he ruled so harshly that the senators, the chief men of the city, determined to rid themselves of him. During an eclipse of the sun, which darkened the city just at the time when Romulus and the senators were assembled in the market-place, the senators fell on the king with their swords and slew him. They then cut his body into small pieces, which they hid beneath their cloaks. When the light returned and the people found that their king had disappeared, the senators told them that Romulus had been carried off by the gods to Mount Olympus, and ordered a temple to be built in his honour on one of the seven hills of Rome.

Mars took the city of Rome under his special protection, and is said to have sent a shield from heaven, during a time of plague, as a sign that he would always watch over the city. The Romans, afraid lest the shield should be stolen, had eleven other shields made, so like the first that only the priests who guarded them in the temple of Mars could tell which was the one sent from heaven. These priests were called Salii, the Leapers, because they danced war dances when, during the month of March, the shields were carried in a procession through the streets of Rome.

To Mars, as the God of War, the Romans naturally turned for help in war-time, and a Roman general, before setting out, went into the temple of Mars and, touching the sacred shield with the point of his spear, cried "Mars, watch over us!"

The training-ground of the Roman soldiers was called Campus Martius (the Field of Mars), in honour of the God of War, and it was commonly believed that Mars himself led their army into battle and helped to give them the victory.

March was named after Mars because of its rough and boisterous weather, and we find the same idea in the minds of the Angles and Saxons, who called it Hlythmonath—the loud or stormy month. Another name for it was Lencten-monath, the lengthening month, because it is during March that the days rapidly become longer.

MARS

From the statue in the Museum delle Terme, Rome

[*Page 27*

CHAPTER IV

April—The Month of Venus

This month of April has only thirty days, which is the number said to have been given to it by Romulus. The king who came after him gave it only twenty-nine, but Cæsar, when he altered the calendar, gave it thirty again.

The name April comes from the Latin word *aperire*, which means "to open", and the month was no doubt so named because it is during April that the earth, which has been bound by the sharp frosts of winter, once again opens beneath the warm rays of the sun; the withered sheaths fall away from the ripened buds, which, opening out, disclose to our eyes their long hidden treasures of beautiful colour.

We find that the month was sacred to Venus, the Roman Goddess of Beauty, and some people think for this reason that the name April comes not from *aperire*, but from *Aphrilis*, which in turn comes from *Aphrodite*, the name given to the Goddess of Beauty by the Greeks.

Venus is said to have sprung from the foam of the sea, and to have made her way to Mount Olympus, the home of the gods, where, because of her wonderful beauty and grace, she was welcomed as the Goddess of Love and Beauty. All the gods fell in love with her, but she scorned them all, and Jupiter, to punish her for her pride, ordered her to marry Vulcan, the God of Fire, who was deformed and very rough in his manner. He had been thrown from the top of Mount Olympus by Jupiter in a fit of anger. Had he not been a god, he would, of course, have been killed by the fall, but he escaped with a broken leg, which made him lame for the rest of his life. He now lived on the earth, and spent his time at the forge making many wonderful and useful things from the metals which he found buried in the mountains. He built gorgeous palaces of gold for the gods, which he decorated with precious stones, forged the terrible thunderbolts used by Jupiter, and also made the arrows used by Venus's son, Cupid. Vulcan was naturally worshipped by all blacksmiths and workers in metal, and a great festival called the Vulcanalia was held in his honour.

Cupid, whom we have just mentioned, was the

God of Love; he never grew up, but remained a little chubby boy, with beautiful wings. He always carried a bow, and with his arrows pierced the hearts of young men and maidens in order to make them fall in love with one another.

Another son of Venus was Æneas, the great hero who was supposed to have been the founder of the Roman race. He escaped from Troy, when at the end of ten years' siege it fell into the hands of the Greeks, and after many adventures reached a part of Italy, called Latium, where in later times his descendants, Romulus and Remus, founded the city of Rome.

The story of Æneas has been wonderfully told by the Roman poet Virgil in his great work called the *Æneid*. In this book Virgil wishes to show that Augustus, the emperor of his time, being a descendant of Æneas, was also descended from the gods, since Æneas was said to be the son of Venus.

Part of the story of Troy, or Ilium, is told in the *Iliad* of Homer, the great Greek poet. We read there of the fierce struggles which took place before the walls of the city, of deeds of strength and valour, and particularly of the final combat between the great heroes Hector the Trojan and Achilles the Greek, in which the Trojan was killed. In spite of many successes in the field, the Greeks were unable to gain an entry into the city, nor were the Trojans able to drive the Greeks from the shore, and it seemed as if neither side would ever secure the victory.

At last Ulysses, a Greek prince who was renowned for his cunning, formed a plan for entering the city and thus finally bringing to an end the war that had lasted for ten years. The Greeks built a wooden horse of such size that a number of men could be hidden within its hollow sides. This horse, filled with fighting men led by Ulysses, was left on the shore, while the army embarked in their ships and sailed away as if tired of the endless struggle. The Greeks also left behind a cunning slave, named Sinon, who was to play an important part in the plot. The Trojans, overjoyed at the departure of the Greeks, flocked down to the shore and crowded round the enormous wooden horse, full of wonderment at its strangeness. Many wished to drag it into the city at once, while some were filled with suspicion and urged their companions to distrust anything made by their enemies. Sinon, when questioned by the Trojans, pretended that he had been ill-treated by the Greeks, and spoke with hatred and anger against them. He explained that the horse was an offering to the sea god, Neptune, whose help the Greeks would need on their journey home, and he advised the Trojans to seize it and take it into the city. In spite even of those who suggested that armed men might be hidden in the horse, the Trojans dragged it into the city with great triumph, pulling down part of the wall to admit it, since it was too large to go through the gates.

Then followed a night of feast and revelry; the Trojans in their excitement laid aside their armour and their weapons, and gave themselves up to wild merrymaking. The smoky flare of the torches lit up a scene of mad delight. Suddenly shouts of alarm arose on every side, followed by the clash of weapons. Armed men poured in on the astonished Trojans, and in a short time Troy was in the hands of the Greeks. Under cover of the darkness and the noise Ulysses and his companions had crept from their hiding-place, had overpowered the careless sentries, and opened the gates for the Greek army, whose ships had returned in the night. Thus, through the help of the clever Ulysses, the Greeks overcame the army that had so often beaten them in the field, and by a trick brought to a victorious end the great Trojan war, for which the Goddess Venus had been responsible, as we shall read in a later chapter.

The Old English name for the month of April was Oster-monath or Easter-monath, because it was the month sacred to Eastre, or Ostara, the Goddess of Spring; the same name is still kept by the Germans, who call it Ostermonath. The time of year known as Easter is named after this goddess, and though Easter is now a Christian festival, it was in the first place a feast held by the Saxons in honour of their goddess Eastre. It was the custom for the people to give one another presents of coloured eggs, because the egg is supposed to represent the beginning of life, and the feast was held in the spring-time, when Nature awakes to a new life from the death of winter. The custom, which we still have, of sending Easter eggs to our friends, is therefore a very, very old one indeed.

CHAPTER V

May—The Month of Maia

This month is named after the goddess Maia, to whom the Romans sacrificed on the first day of the month. Maia was one of the Pleiades, the seven daughters of Atlas and Pleione. They were all transformed into pigeons that they might escape from the great hunter Orion, and flying up into the sky were changed into seven stars, which form the constellation known as the Pleiades. On any clear night you may see these stars clustered closely together, but they are not very bright, one of them being very faint indeed. A story says that at first they shone brightly, but after the capture of Troy by the Greeks they grew pale with sorrow. Another story says that all but one were married to gods, and that when they became stars the one who had married a mortal did not shine so brightly as her sisters.

Maia was the Goddess of the Plains and mother

of Mercury, the messenger of the gods. In order that he might perform his duties as messenger more swiftly, Mercury was given by Jupiter wings for his feet, and a winged cap for his head. He is said to have invented the lyre, or harp, and to have given it to the Sun-god Apollo, who gave him in return a magic wand called Caduceus, which had the power of making enemies become friends. Mercury, in order to test its power, put it between two fighting snakes, and they at once wound themselves round it. Mercury ordered them to stay on the wand, and, in statues and pictures, the god is nearly always holding in his hand this wand with the snakes twisted round it.

Mercury was not only the messenger of the gods, but was also the God of Rain and Wind, and the protector of travellers, shepherds, and thieves. Festivals were held every year in Rome in his honour during the month of May.

Atlas, the father of the Pleiades, was a giant who lived in Africa and held up the sky on his shoulders. The great Hercules, when seeking for the Golden Apples of the Hesperides (daughters of the Evening Star), came to Atlas to ask him where he could find the apples.

Atlas offered to get them for Hercules if he would take his place while he was away, so Hercules took the heavens on his shoulders, and Atlas set off to fetch the golden fruit. But on his return he told Hercules that he must stay where he was, while he himself would take the apples to the king, who had set Hercules the task of finding them. Hercules, as you may imagine, had no wish to spend the rest of his life holding up the sky, and, by a trick, succeeded in getting Atlas back to his place, and so was able to set out on his homeward journey.

The last story of Atlas we read in the account of the great hero Perseus, who, after slaying the Gorgon Medusa, passed Atlas on his way home. Now the face of the Gorgon turned to stone all who looked on it, and Atlas, worn out by the terrible burden he had to bear, persuaded Perseus to show him the Gorgon's head. "Eagerly he gazed for a moment on the changeless countenance, but in an instant the straining eyes were stiff and cold; and it seemed to Perseus, as he rose again into the pale yellow air, that the grey hairs which streamed from the giant's head were like the snow which rests upon the peak of a great mountain, and that, in place of the trembling limbs, he saw only the rents and clefts on a rough hill-side."

Thus Atlas was changed into the mountains which bear his name, and are to be found in the north-west of Africa.

Hercules, whom we have mentioned in this story of Atlas, is one of the best known of the Greek heroes, and to this day we often speak of an especially strong man as a Hercules, and we also have the expression "a Herculean task". Hercules was a son of Jupiter, and devoted his life to ridding the country of the fierce beasts which brought death and destruction to many of his people.   But through the hatred of the goddess Juno, Hercules knew much sorrow, and underwent great trials.   To atone for crimes committed in a fit of madness sent upon him by Juno, he was condemned by the gods to become for a year the slave of the King of Argos, who set him twelve labours.   The first of these labours was to slay a lion known as the Nemean lion. In spite of the attempts of many brave men to kill this fierce animal, it still continued to carry off men and women, and steal cattle and sheep. Hercules at once set out, and, tracking the lion to its den, seized it by the throat and crushed out its life. He then tore off the lion's skin and made it into a covering which he always wore.

The second task was also to destroy a monster —a seven-headed serpent, known as the Hydra. Hercules attacked the serpent with a sword and cut off one of its heads, but was horrified to see seven new heads spring from the wound. Thereupon the hero called to his help his friend Iolaus, who seared the wounds with a lighted torch and thus prevented the new heads from growing. In this way Hercules finally slew the cruel Hydra.

Another task set the hero was to capture and tame the horses of the King of Thrace. These horses were fed on human flesh, and the king had ordered all strangers who entered his kingdom to be executed and given as food to the horses. Hercules succeeded in securing these animals, and, after throwing the king to his own horses as a punishment for his cruelty, led them to his master, the King of Argos.

Of the remaining labours, one was the fetching of the Golden Apples of the Hesperides, which we have mentioned; but the most famous was the cleaning of the Augean stables. King Augeas possessed enormous herds of cattle, and their stables had not been cleaned for many years. Hercules might well have lost heart at the sight of such a task, but he very cleverly overcame the difficulty. Near by the stables ran a swift river; this Hercules dammed and turned from its course, making it run through the stables, which in time it washed perfectly clean. Then, his task accomplished, Hercules led the river back to its course.

After a 'life of trial and labour, Hercules finally met a tragic death. By a trick he was persuaded to put on a robe which had been stained with poison. The poison ate into his flesh, and all the hero's attempts to tear off the robe were in vain, so at last he resolved to die. He built an enormous funeral pyre by tearing up oak trees by the roots, and then laid himself on the pyre, to which one of his friends put a torch. In a short time roaring flames rose up to the sky and consumed the great Hercules, the man of might.

The Angles and Saxons seemed to have called this month of May "Tri-milchi", meaning that, owing to the fresh grass of spring, they were able to milk their cows three times a day.

CHAPTER VI

June—The Month of Juno

The month of June is probably named after Juno, the wife of Jupiter, and queen of the gods. It was held sacred to her, and was thought by the Romans to be the luckiest month for marriage, since Juno was the Goddess of Marriage. Wherever the goddess went she was attended by her messenger Iris (the Rainbow), who journeyed so quickly through the air that she was seldom seen, but after she had passed there was often left in the sky the radiant trail of her highly-coloured robe.

Juno is always represented as a tall, beautiful woman, wearing a crown and bearing a sceptre in her hand, and often she is shown with a peacock at her side, since that bird was sacred to her.

A story is told of one of her servants, Argus,

who had a hundred eyes, only a few of which he closed at a time. Juno set him to watch over a cow which Jupiter wished to steal, for it was really a beautiful girl named Io, whom Jupiter had transformed. Mercury was sent by Jupiter to carry off Io, and by telling long and wearisome stories to Argus at last succeeded in lulling him into so deep a sleep that he closed all his eyes. The god then seized Argus's own sword and cut off his head. Juno was very sad at the loss of her servant, and gathering up his hundred eyes scattered them over the tail of the peacock, her favourite bird.

Juno was of a very jealous disposition, and when angered brought all the misfortune she possibly could on the one who had offended her. At a wedding-feast at which the gods and goddesses were present, Eris, the Goddess of Discord, or Quarrelling, suddenly appeared. She had not been invited because of her evil nature, and in order to have her revenge, she threw on to the table a golden apple bearing the inscription, "To the fairest". A quarrel at once arose as to whom the apple should be given, for it was claimed by Juno, the Queen of Heaven, Minerva, the Goddess of Wisdom, and Venus, the Goddess of

Beauty. Being unable to decide among themselves, they determined to appoint as judge a shepherd named Paris, who was really the son of the King of Troy. The three goddesses appeared before him on a mountain top, and each in turn tried to persuade him by the promise of a great reward. Minerva offered him wisdom and knowledge, Juno offered him wealth and power, while Venus

> " drawing nigh,
> Half-whispered in his ear, ' I promise thee
> The fairest and most loving wife in Greece ' ".

Paris at once gave the apple to Venus, and thus angered Juno and Minerva, who determined to punish him whenever an opportunity occurred. This they were soon able to do, for Paris, prompted by Venus, carried off Helen, the most beautiful woman in all Greece, and brought her to his own city of Troy. This led to the Trojan War, which we have mentioned. The Trojans who made their escape from the city were persecuted by Juno, who brought them into many terrible dangers.

Juno, though jealous and unforgiving, gave ungrudging help to those whom she favoured, and an example of this is seen in the story of Jason and the Golden Fleece. When Jason was a child, his father Æson, had been driven from his kingdom by his brother Pelias, and Jason, as soon as he reached manhood, determined to avenge his father. Accordingly he set out for the court of Pelias, and soon came to a stream much swollen by floods. Knowing no fear, he was about to try to ford the stream, when he saw an old woman on the bank gazing in despair at the foaming waters. He at once offered to help her by taking her on his back, and in spite of the swift stream and his heavy load, succeeded in getting safely across. He lowered the old woman gently to the ground, and was greatly annoyed to find that he had lost one of his sandals in the stream. He turned to bid farewell to the old woman, when she was suddenly transformed into the goddess Juno. Jason begged for her help and protection, which Juno at once promised, and the goddess then vanished. Jason then resumed his journey in all haste, and entering his native city, found Pelias in a temple sacrificing to the gods. He pressed forward through the crowd until he stood close to Pelias, who at length caught sight of this stranger who

JULIUS CÆSAR

From the statue in the National Museum at Naples

[Page 52

seemed anxious to speak to him. Fear at once
filled his heart, for he remembered that it had
been foretold that he should be overthrown by a
man who came to him wearing only one sandal.
Jason stepped forward and boldly claimed the
throne for his father, and Pelias, disguising his
fear and anger, invited him to his palace, where
they could decide the matter. During the ban-
quet which followed, Jason heard the story of
Phrixus and Helle, two children who had escaped
from their cruel stepmother on a winged ram
with a golden fleece, which bore them far away
from their home. As they passed over the sea,
the girl Helle fell from the ram's back into a
part of the sea ever since known as the Helles-
pont (now the Dardanelles). Phrixus reached
Colchis, at the eastern end of the Black Sea,
in safety, and there sacrificed the ram to the
gods and hung its golden fleece on a tree which
stood in a poisonous wood and was guarded by
a serpent. The cunning Pelias dared Jason to
try to win the Golden Fleece, hoping that thus
he would be rid of him for ever. Jason in his
excitement forgot the crime which he had come
to avenge, and recklessly promised to bring the
fleece to Pelias. With the help of Juno, he

amongst them. The warriors thought that they had been struck by one of their own number, with the result that they fell upon each other and fought until they all lay dead on the ground. Medea then led Jason to the tree to which the fleece was fastened, and soothing the terrible serpent by her magic, enabled Jason to cut off its head. He quickly snatched the Golden Fleece from the tree, and with Medea hastened to the shore, whence they set sail in triumph. They wandered far and suffered many misfortunes, but through Juno's help they at last reached their native land. Jason compelled Pelias to give up the kingdom to Æson, who was now an old man. Medea, however, in some strange way was able to restore Æson to his youth and strength, and Pelias' daughters, when they heard of this, asked her how they might do the same for their father. Medea, seeing her opportunity, gave them false instructions, which they followed, only to find that instead of making their father young again they had killed him.

This month of June was called by the Angles and Saxons the "dry month", and sometimes the "earlier mild month"—July being the second mild month.

CHAPTER VII

July—The Month of Julius Cæsar

This month was first called Quintilis, that is, the fifth month, which shows that the year began with March. In the year 44 B.C. the name was changed to Julius in honour of Julius Cæsar, the founder of the Roman Empire. The month Quintilis was chosen as the one to be named after the Emperor Julius because his birthday was on the twelfth of that month After his death, the name Cæsar became a title of the Roman Emperors, and we still have the word in the titles Kaiser of Germany, Czar (or Tsar) of Russia, and Kaisar-i-Hind (Emperor of India), one of the titles of our own king.

Julius Cæsar was a very great soldier, and it was by skill as a general that he became the first emperor the Romans had. Until his time they had no supreme ruler, the chief office being that of consul. There were two consuls who had to be elected, and who only served for a certain length of time. The Romans hated the name of king, and Cæsar, who seemed to have really wished for the title, was afraid to take it, in case it should turn the people against him. In 44 B.C. at the feast of the Lupercalia, held, as we have said, in February, the crown was actually offered to him by Marcus Antonius, a great Roman noble.

> " You all did see that on the Lupercal
> I thrice presented him a kingly crown,
> Which he did thrice refuse."
>
> SHAKESPEARE—*Julius Cæsar.*

Cæsar made himself master of all Italy, conquered the whole of Gaul (i.e. France) and Spain, and won great victories in Greece, Egypt, and Africa. But he is famous not only as a soldier; he was a great statesman, a great orator, and a clever writer and historian. He formed several plans for the improvement of Roman life, and took a great interest in the building of public works. He reformed the calendar, as we have seen, and he wished to have the Roman law set out in a clear way, so that it could be easily understood; he had plans for draining marsh land near Rome in order to make the country more healthy, for enlarging the harbour of Ostia, a very important port near Rome, and for making a canal through the Isthmus of Corinth in Greece.

In the year 44 B.C., before he could carry out any of these very useful plans, he was killed in Rome by men who had once been his friends, but were now jealous of his power. Shakespeare describes this tragedy in his play *Julius Cæsar*, and makes Marcus Antonius, when looking upon the murdered Cæsar, say:

> "Thou art the ruins of the noblest man
> That ever lived in the tide of times".

Cæsar is particularly interesting to us because he came to our island in the days of the Ancient Britons. In one of his books he tells us that there were great numbers of people, many buildings, and much cattle. There were trees of every kind, as in Gaul, except the beech and the fir.

"The hare, the hen, and the goose they do not think it right to eat, but they keep them for amusement and pleasure. Most of those living inland do not sow corn, but live on milk and flesh, and are clothed in skins. All stain themselves with woad, which gives a blue colour, and makes them of more hideous appearance in battle. They have long hair, but shave every part of their body except the head and upper lip."

At the time of Cæsar's invasion London was a stronghold of the Britons, and was very probably attacked and captured by Cæsar. The first mention of London in history is in a book by a Roman historian named Tacitus, who, in describing what happened in the year A.D. 61, tells us that the Roman general leading the army here in Britain was unable to hold the town at the time of Boadicea's revolt. London was then very largely destroyed, but the Romans rebuilt it and gave it a new name, Augusta, in honour of their Emperor Augustus. This shows that it was a place of great importance even in those early days.

The days from 3rd July to 11th August, 'the hottest part of the year, were called by the Romans, "dog-days", because they thought the great heat was due to Sirius, the dog-star. Sirius was a dog belonging to the giant Orion, who was a great hunter. Diana, the Goddess of the Moon, was also the Goddess of Hunting, and after she had driven her chariot with its white horses across the starlit sky, she spent the day hunting in the forests. Here she often met Orion, and soon fell in love with him. This angered her brother Apollo, the sun-god, who determined to put an end to their friendship. One day he called Diana to him, and began to talk about her skill as an archer. Pretending that he wished to test her skill, he asked her to shoot at a dark speck which could be seen floating far out at sea. Diana, all unsuspecting, at once drew her bow, and so strong and true was her aim that she hit the object, which disappeared beneath the waves. She then found that the dark speck was the head of Orion, who had been cooling himself in the sea after his hunting. She was filled with grief at his death, and vowing never to forget him, placed him and his dog Sirius in the sky. The constellation Orion can easily be found on a clear night, for the stars forming his belt and sword are unmistakable. Following behind the giant is the very bright star Sirius — "the scorching flames of fierce Orion's hound". Virgil in his *Æneid* describes one of the heroes of Latium as being "as great as Orion, who, walking on foot through the deep waters of the very middle of the sea, making himself a path, yet rises above the billows with his shoulders; or carrying down an ancient ash from the summit of the mountains, has his feet on the earth, his head shrouded by the clouds of heaven".

The Angles and Saxons had two names for this month of July: Hegmonath, the hay-month, and Maedmonath, the mead-month. A third name was sometimes given to it—the "latter mild month", that is, the second warm month.

CHAPTER VIII

August—The Month of Augustus

This month is also named after a great Roman emperor, Augustus Cæsar, but was first called Sextilis, the sixth month. Augustus, whose full name was Caius Julius Cæsar Octavianus — Augustus (the Majestic) being a title given him after he became emperor—was a young man at the time of Cæsar's murder. Julius, who had no son of his own, adopted Augustus as his son and heir, in order that when he died Augustus should become emperor in his place. The nobles who had killed Julius, however, did not wish Augustus to become emperor, and it was not until he had fought and won many battles that he became the head of the Roman Empire. As soon as he had conquered all his enemies, he returned to Rome, and, closing the temple of Janus, proclaimed peace throughout the Empire. During his reign there lived the greatest poets and

writers that Rome ever had, of whom the best
known are Virgil, Horace, Ovid, and Livy; just
as in the reign of our Queen Elizabeth there
lived some of England's greatest poets and
writers — in fact the time from Spenser and
Sidney in Elizabeth's reign, passing beyond
Shakespeare to Milton in Charles II's reign, is
spoken of as the "Augustan Age" of English
Literature.

The month known as Sextilis was chosen as
the one to be named after Augustus, because it
was during that month that the most fortunate
events of his life had happened.   In that month
he had first become consul, the most important
man in Rome; he had three times entered the
city in triumph after his great victories; he had
conquered Egypt and had ended the civil wars.
As the month had only thirty days, and the one
named after Julius Cæsar had thirty-one, a day
was taken from February in order to make them
equal.

We have more than once mentioned the poet
Virgil's most famous work, the *Æneid*, in which he
describes the wanderings of Æneas, who gathered
together all that was left of the Trojan army and
escaped from the fallen city, carrying his father

Anchises on his back, since he was old and weak
and unable to walk. The fugitives reached the
shore in safety and sailed away from their ruined
country. But the goddess Juno, not satisfied
by the death of Paris and the disaster which had
fallen on the Trojans, pursued Æneas and his
followers with her hatred, and again and again
brought them into misfortune. They wandered
from country to country for many years, seeking
a spot where they might settle down in peace
and safety, but Juno gave them no rest. She
brought sickness upon them so that many died,
and sent fierce storms which scattered their fleet
and destroyed many of their ships. At last they
reached a harbour on the coast of Africa, and
made their way to a city which they found to
be Carthage. Æneas was welcomed by Dido,
the queen of the city, who listened eagerly to
the story of his adventures. Now, Æneas had
been destined by the gods to found a new kingdom, when his wanderings finally came to an
end, but the time was not yet. The goddess
Venus caused Dido to fall in love with Æneas,
and the hero, happy in her love and the pleasant
life of her court, lingered on. A year passed,
and the gods at length sent Mercury to remind

Æneas of his destiny. Æneas' heart sank at the thought of leaving the beautiful Dido, and afraid of her anger, he secretly set sail one dark night while the queen was sleeping. When Dido discovered her loss she was filled with grief. She ordered her servants to make a funeral pyre on which was placed an effigy of her lover, and then setting fire to the pyre with her own hand, she sprang into the flames and perished.

Æneas and his companions sailed on till they reached the Island of Sicily, where they took refuge from a storm. During a festival which the men then held in honour of Anchises, Æneas' father, who had died just a year before, Juno stirred up the women to revolt against their hard life. Tired of their perilous wanderings, they gathered on the shore and set fire to the ships. Æneas, when he heard of this new disaster, rushed down to the shore, and cried to Jupiter for help. In answer to the prayer, the King of the Gods sent a storm of rain, which put out the destroying flames. The Trojans then left Sicily, and, coming to Italy, to the mouth of the River Tiber, they followed the river until they reached the country of Latium. Here they were well received by the king, Latinus, who offered to Æneas the hand of his daughter Lavinia. Lavinia, however, had many suitors, the chief of whom was Turnus, the prince of a neighbouring country, and Juno once again interfered by stirring up the people of Latium against Æneas, with the result that Latinus made war on his former friend. Turnus led the army against the Trojans, and performed great deeds of valour, which were only matched by those of Æneas. While Juno was assisting Turnus in every possible way, Venus was not forgetful of her son Æneas, and she obtained from Vulcan, the God of Fire, a wonderful suit of armour, which enabled Æneas to do even mightier deeds. Turnus and Æneas at length met in single combat, and, after a fierce encounter, Turnus was killed. Peace was made with Latinus, and Æneas married Lavinia. He founded a city, which he called Lavinia, and his descendants reigned in Latium for many years. It was one of his race, the Vestal Ilia, who married Mars and became the mother of Romulus and Remus, the founders of Rome.

One of the famous passages in the *Æneid* is the description of the shield given to Æneas by the goddess Venus. On this shield Vulcan,

knowing the future, had depicted the history of
the descendants of Æneas, and had foretold the
glory of Rome. He showed the wolf nursing
the two sons of Mars and Ilia, the wars which
followed the founding of Rome, and the brave
Horatius, who defended the bridge over the
Tiber against the army of Tarquin. With
wonderful skill he pictured the sacred geese
giving warning to the Romans of the approach
of the Gauls in the dead of night. "Manlius
stood before the temple and kept the lofty
Capitol; a silver goose flitting through arches of
gold gave warning with its cries that the Gauls
were on the threshold; the Gauls were drawing
near through the bushes, and were grasping the
Citadel, protected by the darkness and the favour
of a gloomy night. Their hair is golden and
their dress of gold, their cloaks are striped, their
milk-white necks are encircled with bands of
gold; each brandishes in his hand two Alpine
javelins, and their bodies are protected by their
long shields." In the middle of the shield
Vulcan had depicted the famous sea-battle of
Actium, in which the Emperor Augustus overthrew his enemies, and finally he showed the
emperor seated at the entrance to the Temple of

AUGUSTUS CÆSAR

From the statue in the Vatican Museum, Rome

[*Page 58*

CHAPTER IX

September—The Seventh Month

The name of this month means simply "seventh", and so suggests to us neither god nor hero. We find, however, that there were seve al festivals held in the month, and not the least important of these was one held on the second of the month, and known as the Actian Games. On this day, in the year 31 B.C., was fought the great sea battle, off Actium in Greece, in which Augustus defeated Marcus Antonius and the Egyptian queen Cleopatra. On the promontory of Actium stood a temple to Apollo, and from that time onward games in honour of Apollo were held on each anniversary of the victory. It was a common custom among the Greeks and Romans to hold games or sports in honour of a god, and the most famous of all, the Olympic Games, were held every four years in Greece in honour of Zeus, the Roman Jupiter. These games lasted for five days, and consisted of foot-races, chariot-races, wrestling, boxing, throwing the quoit and the javelin. The first prize was usually a wreath made from the laurel tree, the favourite tree of Apollo. A story says that Apollo fell in love with Daphne, a beautiful wood-nymph and daughter of a river-god. Daphne, however, did not return Apollo's love, and on one occasion ran away from him. The sun-god pursued her, calling to her that he meant no harm, but just as he was within reach of her she prayed to her father for help. She at once became rooted to the ground, and found that her limbs were rapidly changing into branches and her hair into leaves. When Apollo stretched out his hands to catch her, he found nothing in his grasp but the trunk of a tree. The river-god had changed his daughter into a laurel. From that time onward Apollo took the laurel for his favourite tree, and said that prizes given to poets and musicians—for Apollo was also god of music and poetry—should be wreaths made from the leaves of that tree. Thus the laurel wreath came to be more eagerly sought after than gold or silver.

The Olympic Games which we have mentioned are the origin of the Olympic Games which have been held in Europe and America every fourth year for some years past. They are held at the capital of each of the great countries in turn, and they were held in London at the Shepherd's Bush Exhibition in 1908. The chief event is the Marathon Race, which in 1908 was run from Windsor to the Stadium at the Exhibition, a distance of 25 miles. This race has its origin in an historical event of the year 490 B.C. In that year was fought the great battle of Marathon between the Greeks and the invading Persians. In spite of the far greater numbers of the Persian army, the Greeks won a glorious victory. Now, in the ranks of the Greek army was a famous runner named Pheidippides, who had won many a prize in the Games. When the Persians had been put to flight, the Greek general sent for Pheidippides and bade him run with the news of the victory to Athens (the capital of Greece), distant nearly 25 miles, where all those unable to fight were awaiting anxiously the result of the battle. Pheidippides, although tired by his share in the battle, at once set off on his long journey. In time the strain of the task began to tell upon him, and it was only by a great effort that he was able to continue his course. At last, with aching limbs and faltering step, he came in sight of the city. The Athenians, seeing him in the distance, ran eagerly to meet him; falling into the arms of the foremost of them, the runner with his last breath gasped, " Rejoice, we conquer". Even as the joyful words left his lips, Pheidippides sank lifeless in the arms that held him, and his brave spirit went forth on its last journey to meet the Heroes of the Past.

" So, when Persia was dust, all cried, ' To Akropolis!
Run, Pheidippides, one race more! the meed is thy due!
"Athens is saved, thank Pan," go shout!' He flung down his shield
Ran like fire once more: and the space 'twixt the Fennel-field
And Athens was stubble again, a field which a fire runs through,
Till in he broke: ' Rejoice, we conquer!' Like wine through clay,
Joy in his blood bursting his heart, he died—the bliss!"
ROBERT BROWNING—Pheidippides.

Famous among the very old stories of the Greeks is that of the swift-footed Atalanta, the daughter of the King of Arcadia. This king had longed for a son who might succeed him, and on the birth of Atalanta was filled with anger and disappointment. He ordered her to be taken away while she was still a baby, and left on a mountain top at the mercy of the wild beasts. Here she was found by some hunters, who took pity on her and carried her to their home. As she grew up, they taught her to hunt, and in time she became more skilled in running and in the chase than they all. She took part with some of the great heroes in a famous hunt for a wild boar, which she finally helped to kill. Her father, hearing of her skill, welcomed her back, and since he still had no son, urged her to marry one of the many suitors who came to the court. Atalanta, however, had no desire to marry, and knowing that she could run more swiftly than any of those who sought her hand in marriage, she declared that she would only marry the man who could outrun her. She also decreed that every one who failed to win should pay for his defeat with his life. In spite of these cruel conditions, many eager youths tried to win her, but she outran them all, and their heads were exposed on the race-course in order to frighten others who might wish to marry her.

At last there came to the court of the King of Arcadia a young man named Milanion, who was determined to win Atalanta for his wife. He had previously sought the help and protection of Venus, and in answer to his prayer the goddess had given him three golden apples. The proud Atalanta accepted Milanion's challenge, and once again the course was thronged with people eager to see the daring youth. The signal was given, and the runners darted forward. Atalanta soon passed Milanion, who then threw at her feet one of his golden apples. She paused a moment, tempted by the glittering object, then stooping, she quickly snatched it up and raced after Milanion, who was by this time ahead of her. She soon overtook him, when he threw down a second golden apple, and again she stopped to pick it up. A third time the swift maiden passed the youth, once more to be tempted by the golden fruit. Sure of her skill, she paused to seize the third golden apple, but before she could overtake Milanion he had reached the goal. Atalanta, bound by her promise, consented to marry the victorious Milanion, and their wedding was celebrated amid great rejoicing.

The Old-English name for September was "Gerstmonath", which means "barley month", since during September the barley crop was usually harvested.

CHAPTER X

October—The Eighth Month

In this, the "eighth" month, was held a great festival at Eleusis, a town twelve miles from Athens, in honour of the Greek goddess Demeter. The Roman name for Demeter was Ceres, and she was worshipped as the Goddess of Agriculture, since the fields and their crops were thought to be under her special care. The Greek name Demeter means "Earth Mother", and the name Ceres has given us the word "cereals", a general name for wheat, barley, rye, and oats.

Ceres had a daughter, Persephone, who spent a great part of her time wandering with her companions on the slopes and plains of Sicily. One day, as Persephone and her maidens were plucking flowers and weaving them into garlands, Pluto, the God of the Underworld, rode by in his dark chariot drawn by four black horses. Attracted by Persephone's beauty, he determined to carry her off and make her his queen.

One story says that he caused a most wonderful flower to spring up, and Persephone, seeing it in the distance and wishing to gather it, was thus separated from her companions. As she stooped to pluck the flower the earth opened, and Pluto in his chariot came up from the Underworld and, seizing Persephone, carried her down to his dark and gloomy home.

Another story says that as soon as he saw Persephone he walked quickly towards her, and before she could guess his intention, caught her up and, carrying her in spite of her struggles to his chariot, drove away at topmost speed. He at length reached a river, whose roaring torrent it was impossible to cross. Afraid to turn back lest he should meet Ceres, he struck the earth such a blow with the two-pronged fork which he always carried as the emblem of his power, that the ground opened beneath him, and thus he was able to reach his dark kingdom of Hades in safety. This Hades, the Underworld to which Pluto had brought Persephone, was the home of the dead, the place to which came the spirits of those who had died, there to receive a fitting reward for their deeds on earth.

From Pluto's throne flowed five rivers:

1. Styx (the Hateful), a sacred river, and one by which the gods "fear to swear, and not keep their oath". It was also the river which had to be crossed by the spirits before they could reach the throne. They were ferried across by an old boatman named Charon, who charged them an obol, about $1\frac{1}{2}d$. of our money. It was the custom, when a man died, for his relations to put an obol under his tongue, so that he might have no difficulty in crossing the Styx. Those who came without their obol had to wait a hundred years, after which time Charon would take them across free of charge.

2. Acheron (Pain), a dark and very deep river that also had to be crossed by the spirits.

3. Lethe (Forgetfulness), which had the power of making all those who drank of its waters forget the past.

4. Phlegethon (Blazing), a river of fire which surrounded Tartarus, that part of the Underworld to which were sent the spirits of evil-doers, in order that they might suffer punishment for their wicked deeds.

5. Cocytus (Wailing), a river of salt water, the tears of those condemned to the torments of Tartarus.

In a distant part of Hades, far removed from the place of torment, were the Elysian Fields. Here dwelt the great and the good, in perpetual day, and amid the ever-blooming flowers of an eternal spring.

While the frightened Persephone was thus, against her will, made queen of this sunless kingdom of the dead, Ceres, with many tears, was seeking her daughter in the flower-strewn meadows, but all in vain. After many wanderings in Italy, and even in Greece, where she visited the city of Eleusis mentioned above, Ceres at last learnt of Persephone's fate, but her joy at finding that she was safe was turned to grief by the thought that Pluto would never allow her to come back to the happiness of the sun-lit earth.

Meanwhile the goddess had neglected all her duties; the flowers withered away, the trees shed their leaves, the fruit was fast falling from the branches, and the crops could not ripen. The time of harvest was quickly passing, and the people, threatened with famine, and finding that their prayers to the goddess were unheeded, appealed to Jupiter to save them from starvation and death by allowing Persephone to return to the upper world. Jupiter at last consented, and said that Pluto must give up Persephone, provided that she had not eaten anything since the time when she had been carried off. Unfortunately that very day she had tasted a pomegranate which Pluto had given her, and she was compelled to stay with her husband one month for each of the six seeds she had eaten. So for six months she has to live in the Underworld, and there in the thick gloom, never pierced by a ray of sunshine, she waits for the time when she may return to the sun-kissed hills and plains of her favourite land, where, happy in her mother's smile, she dances with her companions amid the flowers.

" Persephone to Ceres has returned
   From that dark god who stole her for his bride,
   And bids the Earth, that for her coming yearned,
   Its sombre garb of mourning lay aside.
   The sun o'ertops the clouds with wonted speed,
   And so to give the goddess honour due,
   O'er hill and dale, o'er mountain-side and mead,
   Now scatters flowers of many a wondrous hue.
   The trees that shed their leaves, each leaf a tear,
   Now deck themselves again in bright array,

And Man delights to see the Winter drear
Yield place to Spring, and Night to gladsome Day."

At length comes the time when once more
Persephone must return to her desolate home,
and with heavy heart she leaves the sorrowing
Ceres.

" Persephone is called away,
    And Ceres weeps
That she must go; while o'er the Earth
    Now slowly creeps
The gloom of death; fled is that smile
    Of love that made
All Nature waken into life,
    And all things fade."

The Old - English name for October was
"Winterfylleth", that is, "winter full moon",
because winter was supposed to begin at the
October full moon.

CHAPTER XI

November—The Ninth Month

On the thirteenth of this "ninth" month the Romans held a feast in honour of Jupiter, the ruler of gods and men. From the clouded top of Mount Olympus he held sway over the whole world, and even the gods had to bow to his supreme will. Terrible indeed was it to anger any of the gods, but no punishment was more swift and sure than that sent by Jupiter when he was enraged. We have seen how with his thunderbolt he slew the proud and reckless Phaeton, and we have another example in the story of Bellerophon. This hero, who was staying at the court of a Grecian king, was set the task of killing the Chimæra, a terrible monster with a lion's head, a goat's body, a dragon's tail, and breath of fire. While sorrowfully wondering how he could possibly perform so difficult a task, Bellerophon suddenly found before him the goddess Minerva, who asked him the cause of his trouble. As soon as she had learnt of his task she promised to help him, and, giving him a golden bridle, told him to bridle the horse Pegasus.

Now Pegasus was a winged horse which the sea-god Neptune had made from the drops of blood that fell into the sea from the head of the Gorgon Medusa, slain by Perseus. He was perfectly white and of great speed, and, as Bellerophon well knew, came down to earth to drink at a certain spring. Bellerophon waited in hiding by this spring, and taking Pegasus by surprise, jumped upon his back. The winged horse at once flew up to a great height, trying to unseat Bellerophon; but the hero succeeded in putting on Minerva's golden bridle, when Pegasus at once became gentle. Bellerophon then set off on his task, and suddenly swooping down from the sky upon the Chimæra, overcame and killed the dreadful monster. His task accomplished, he might now have lived in happiness, but he became filled with pride because of the wonderful flights he had made on Pegasus. One day, as he soared up higher and higher, he began to think himself equal to the gods, and wished to join them on Mount Olympus. This angered Jupiter, who sent a gadfly which stung Pegasus. Suddenly rearing up, the winged horse threw the proud Bellerophon far down to the earth beneath.

The goddess, Minerva, who appeared to Bellerophon, was a daughter of Jupiter, but she was born in a very strange way, for she sprang out of her father's head, clothed in bright armour, and with a spear in her hand. She became the Goddess of Wisdom (as we have seen in the story of Paris), of the arts and the sciences, and of spinning and weaving. Her skill in weaving is shown by the following story.

There once lived in Greece a girl named Arachne, who was so clever at needlework that at last in her pride she boasted that she could weave more skilfully than Minerva herself. Minerva, angered by these words, one day came down to Arachne's home, and accepted the challenge which she had so rashly made. The story is thus told by the poet Spenser in "The Fate of the Butterflie":

> " Minerva did the challenge not refuse,
> But deigned with her the paragon to make;
> So to their work they sit, and each doth choose
> What story she will for her tapet[1] take ".

[1] Tapet, i.e. tapestry.

Arachne pictured the story of Jupiter when, disguised as a white bull, he carried off Europa to the land which afterwards bore the name Europe. Minerva chose for her work the story of her own contest with the sea-god Neptune as to which of them should have the honour of naming a new city that had been built in Greece. Jupiter had said that the honour would be given to the one who gave the most useful gift to man, and he called all the gods together to judge the contest. Neptune struck the ground with his trident and there sprang forth a horse. The gods were filled with wonder at the sight of the noble animal, and when Neptune explained how useful it would be to man, they all thought that the victory would be his. Minerva then produced an olive tree; at this all the gods laughed with scorn, but when the goddess, heedless of their laughter, had explained how all its parts—the wood, the fruit, and the leaves—could be used by man, how it was the sign of peace while the horse was the symbol of war, they decided that Minerva had won, and since her name among the Greeks was Athene, she gave to the city the name of Athens.

All this the goddess wove in her tapestry:

PHŒBUS APOLLO

From the painting by Briton Riviere, R.A.   By permission of the Art Gallery Committee
of the Corporation of Birmingham

The artist here shows the car of "the lord of life and light" drawn by lions, his mastery of which may be taken
as typifying the power of the sun over all living things.

[Page 94

" Then sets she forth, how with her weapon dread
   She smote the ground, the which straight forth did
      yield
   A fruitful Olive tree, with berries spread,
   That all the gods admired: then all the story
   She compassed with a wreath of Olives hoary.

   Amongst the leaves she made a Butterfly,
   With excellent device and wondrous sleight,
   Flutt'ring among the Olives wantonly,
   That seemed to live, so like it was in sight;
   The velvet nap which on his wings doth lie,
   The silken down with which his back is dight,
   His broad outstretched horns, his hairy thighs,
   His glorious colours, and his glistering eyes.

   Which when Arachne saw, as overlaid
   And mastered with workmanship so rare,
   She stood astonied long, nor ought gainsaid;
   And with fast-fixed eyes on her did stare,
   And by her silence, sign of one dismayed,
   The victory did yield her as her share."

Then in anger and despair, the unhappy girl
hanged herself, and Minerva turned her dangling
body into a spider, and bade her for ever spin
and weave.

The Angles and Saxons had two names for
this month of November: " Windmonath ", that

is, "wind month", and "Blodmonath", that is, "blood month". The latter name arose from the fact that during this month they slaughtered large numbers of cattle to last them through the cold and dreary winter.

CHAPTER XII

December—The Tenth Month

The chief festival of this "tenth" and last month of the Roman year was the Saturnalia, held on the seventeenth of the month in honour of Saturn, the father of Jupiter. Saturn, or Cronos, as the Greeks called him, was one of the Titans, the six giant sons of Uranus (Heaven) and Gaia (Earth). Uranus ruled before the days of Man, but he was overthrown by his son Saturn, who became for a time the supreme ruler of the universe. Uranus, however, prophesied that Saturn would one day himself be overthrown by his children, and in order to avoid this, Saturn, when his first child was born, immediately swallowed him! As other children were born, he swallowed each of them, until at last Rhea, his wife, succeeded in hiding her youngest son, Jupiter, and deceived Saturn by giving him a stone wrapped in swaddling clothes, which, in his haste, he swallowed without realizing the trick played upon him. Jupiter was thus saved, and when he grew up he overthrew his father, as Uranus had foretold. Saturn, having lost his power, took refuge on the Earth, and became king of a part of Italy, which, as Virgil tells us in the eighth book of his *Æneid*, he called Latium, since it was there that he lay hid (Latin: *lateo* = to lie hidden). "Saturn was the first to come from heavenly Olympus, fleeing the arms of Jupiter, an exile deprived of his kingdom. He it was who made into a nation a people untaught and scattered on the mountain tops, and gave them laws, and chose that the land should be called 'Latium' because in safety he had lain hidden in this region."

Jupiter's rule was very soon threatened by the Titans, who refused to bow to his will, but after a long and terrible struggle, the giants were overthrown by Jupiter's thunderbolts. One of the giants was imprisoned under Mount Ætna, where, breathing out fire and smoke, he still struggles to free himself, thus causing earthquakes and volcanic eruptions.

Another of the Titans, Iapetus, had two sons, Prometheus (Forethought) and Epimetheus

(Afterthought). To these two gods fell the task of making man, who was to rule over all living creatures. Prometheus was very anxious to give to the race of men that he had fashioned a power that would make them supreme on the earth, and nearer to the gods themselves. The way in which he could best bestow this power upon them was by the gift of fire, for fire belonged only to the gods and was jealously guarded by them. In spite of the terrible punishment which he knew awaited him should he be discovered, Prometheus determined to steal fire from heaven, and during one dark night he brought down to the earth a burning stick from the home of the gods on Mount Olympus. Jupiter, seeing an unaccustomed light on the earth, discovered the theft, and his rage knew no bounds. He seized Prometheus, carried him off to the Caucasus Mountains, and there bound him with chains to a huge rock. Then he sent a vulture that, day after day, might feed upon his liver, which grew again during the night so that the terrible torture of the god should have no end. After hundreds of years of this ghastly pain and suffering, Prometheus was rescued by Hercules, who came to him to ask him where he might find the

Golden Apples of the Hesperides.   Hercules killed the vulture, broke Prometheus' chains, and released the tortured god, who in return advised Hercules to go to the giant Atlas, who knew where the apples were, as we have seen in the story of Atlas' daughter, Maia.

Prometheus' brother, Epimetheus, married the beautiful Pandora, and at first lived with her in great happiness, for in those early days the earth was free from pain, sickness, and ills of every kind.   One evening they saw Mercury, the messenger of the gods, coming towards them and bearing on his shoulder a huge box which seemed to be of great weight.   Tired out with his burden, Mercury begged permission to leave the box to their care, promising to return for it in a short time.   Pandora and Epimetheus readily granted permission, and Mercury placed the box in their house and hastily departed. Pandora was at once filled with great curiosity as to what the box might contain, and suggested to Epimetheus that they should just peep inside. Epimetheus was shocked by Pandora's lack of good manners, and, replying that they must not think of such a thing, he went out, calling to Pandora to follow him.   But Pandora's curiosity was now thoroughly aroused, and the temptation overcame her when she found herself alone. Quickly she undid the cord which bound the box, and, thinking she heard sounds in the box, she put her ear close to the lid. To her surprise she heard voices calling, "Let us out! let us out!" Pandora, filled with excitement, slowly raised the lid a little, just for a peep, as she said to herself. But no sooner was the box opened than out flew little winged creatures, some of which settled on Pandora and Epimetheus, who had now returned, and stung them so that they knew pain for the first time. Then escaping into the world, these insects, Evil, Sickness, Unhappiness, and all the little troubles of life, became a cause of endless pain and suffering to men and women. Poor Pandora was broken hearted, and her eyes filled with tears at the thought of the harm she had done. Then again she was startled to hear a voice still calling from the box. It sounded so kind and gentle and pleaded so sweetly to be let out, that Pandora raised the lid a second time, and out flew Hope, who had been shut in with the cruel insects, and now fluttered busily over the earth, healing the wounds made by her evil companions.

This cheery little creature, Hope, may well be associated with the winter month December, when Ceres and her trees and flowers mourn for the smiling Persephone, yet cling to the hope of her return. It is Hope who bids us say with the poet, "If Winter comes, can Spring be far behind?"

On December 25th, the Romans held a festival of the winter solstice, the turning point of winter, when the days begin to grow longer. It was called *Dies Natalis Solis Invicti* (the Birthday of the Unconquered Sun), and it is very probable that for this reason the Christians chose the 25th of December for the birthday of Christ. In early times Christmas (the Mass or Feast of Christ) was kept at different times in the year, but it was finally fixed on December 25th, since on that day there was already held this heathen festival to the sun, which had a meaning in some way similar to that of our Christmas. It was an easy thing to make the Birthday of the Unconquered Sun, which wakes all nature from its winter sleep, into the Birthday of the Unconquered Son of God, who brought new life and hope to the world.

The same thing took place among the northern

races of Europe and in our own islands. The first Christian missionaries found that, at the time of year we now call Christmas, the Northmen kept a festival called Yule, the greatest feast in the year. "Yule" means "wheel", and the festival was so named because the sun was thought to be like a wheel revolving swiftly across the sky. It used at one time to be a custom in England and Germany for the people to gather each year on a hill-top, to set fire to a huge wooden wheel bound with straw, and to send it rolling down the hill. The Christians made this festival into a Christian festival, and we still speak of Christmas as Yuletide. The origin of Santa Claus is St. Nicholas, who was the patron saint of Russia. He was famous for his kindness and generosity, and a festival was held in his honour on the 6th of December.

The custom of giving "Christmas boxes" comes from the Romans, and in later days these gifts came to be called "boxes", because at Christmas time boxes were hung up in the churches in which people might put money for the poor. On the day after Christmas Day these boxes were opened, and the day was thus known as "Boxing Day". Another custom

CHAPTER XIII

Stories of the Days

The days of the week are as full of story as the months, but they take us away from the sunlit countries of Greece and Rome to the cold and stormy lands of the Northmen. They are really of greater interest to us, because four of these days are named after gods worshipped by the Angles and Saxons. Sunday and Monday are named after the sun and the moon, which have been worshipped from the beginning of time in all lands and by all peoples, but Tuesday, Wednesday, Thursday, and Friday remind us of the great gods who reigned in the lands across the North Sea, lands of biting frost and freezing winds. Our ancestors were a brave and hardy race, and not even the dangers of the stormy seas could check their eagerness for adventure, as we know. They were great fighters, and even thought it a disgrace to die what they called a "straw death", that is, to die in their beds of straw instead of on the field of battle. As we should expect, their gods were great fighters too, and many stirring tales are told of the gods and of the great heroes among men. Songs of the gods and their creation of the world, and songs of the deeds of the heroes, were composed in very early times by poets and handed down by word of mouth. These songs, known as Eddas and Sagas, were eventually written down, the earliest of them in the thirteenth century. In these poems we find a description of the gods and goddesses of the Northmen and of their enemies the frost giants, an account of the creation of the world, and stories of the adventures that befell both gods and giants. The following chapters contain the stories which are suggested by the names Tiu, Woden, Thor, and Freya, after whom Tuesday, Wednesday, Thursday, and Friday are named, while Saturday suggests to us the great day of Ragnarok, the downfall of the gods, when the gods were overthrown by the powers of evil and the earth was destroyed, and new gods and a new earth rose in their place.

CHAPTER XIV

Sunday—The Day of the Sun

Among all peoples in early times the sun was an object of wonder. It was to them a mystery, but although they could never understand it, they imagined many explanations of it. When we remember that in those long-ago days nothing was known of the rotation of the earth or of its movement round the sun, we can readily see how very real the movement of the sun must have seemed. But if it moved across the sky it must be a chariot, for it was in chariots that all men travelled quickly, while none but a god could ride across the sky.

The nature of the sun may have been difficult to understand, but the comforts and the benefits which it brought to men were plain to all. It was a kindly god who gave the earth warmth and light, who ripened the crops and the fruit and made them serviceable to man, who clothed the trees with leaves and scattered the fields with flowers. It is little wonder then that in all parts of the world men worshipped the sun, and the god whom they pictured in their imagination was all the more real to them because of the great work he performed.

We have seen how the Greeks and Romans worshipped the sun as Apollo, the god who set out each day when the Gates of the East had been opened by the Goddess of the Dawn, and, driving his chariot across the sky, dipped down into the ocean, where a boat awaited him to bring him back. Apollo was the most beautiful of the gods, as befitted the giver of light and happiness, and was worshipped throughout those sunny lands of the South. On the Island of Rhodes, off the coast of Asia Minor, stood one of the Seven Wonders of the World, a statue of Apollo. It was known as the Colossus of Rhodes on account of its size, for it was 100 feet high, the fingers of the god being as long as a man. It was placed at the entrance to a harbour, and remained in position for nearly sixty years, and was then (224 B.C.) overthrown by an earthquake.

The principal temples of Apollo were in the

Island of Delos, and at Delphi in Greece, and it was at this town of Delphi that the great Pythian Games were held every four years in honour of the god. The games were so called because Apollo was believed to have slain at Delphi a dragon called Python.

The sun's daily journey, his contest with the darkness, and his final victory at the dawn of the new day are ideas which have led to endless stories, and we find these stories are very similar among different peoples. Ra, the great sun-god of Egypt, was pictured as travelling by day in a ship across the waters of the sky, and returning during the night through the kingdom of the dead. To the Egyptians Ra was a symbol of life, death, and a new birth or resurrection. Through the night Ra fought with the lord of the powers of darkness, a huge serpent, who awaited the sun in the west with a band of demons, and whom he overcame at the approach of dawn. Ra was always represented either as a hawk or as a man with a hawk's head, with the sun on his head. The hawk was chosen as his symbol, because it was said to fly towards the sun.

In India the sun was worshipped as the god

Agni, who rode in a shining chariot drawn by blood-red horses. He was golden-haired, and had a double face, seven tongues, and seven arms.

Among the gods of the early British who were driven into Ireland was the sun-god Nudd, or Ludd, as he was sometimes called. His name appears in Ludgate, and it is thought that his temple stood on what is now Ludgate Hill in London. At a town called Lydney, in Gloucestershire, the remains of a temple to Ludd have been found, with many inscriptions containing his name.

The Angles and Saxons imagined the sun to be carried in a chariot driven by a maiden named Sol, as we shall read later. They had no god whom we can describe exactly as a sun-god, but several of their gods were like the sun in many ways, particularly Frey, whose sword sent out rays of light like the sun, and who caused the crops to ripen, and Balder the Beautiful, the God of Light, who was the favourite son of Odin, father of the gods, and was, as his name shows, the most handsome of the gods, ever happy and light-hearted. His golden hair and his bright, clear eyes shone like the sun, and his radiant smile warmed the hearts of all who met him. He knew no thought of evil, but was "good and pure, and bright, was loved by all, as all love light".

In spite of his lovable nature, however, Balder was destined to misfortune through his twin brother, Hodur, the God of Darkness, who was the exact opposite of his brother, for he was gloomy and silent, and suffered from blindness. Odin, through his great wisdom, knew that disaster was to come to Balder, and spared no effort to stave off the evil day, by making all things in creation swear that they would never harm the God of Light. This they were only too ready to do, and all made a solemn vow, with the one exception of a shoot of mistletoe, which was passed over as being too slight a thing ever to cause harm to anyone. Balder being now free from all possibility of hurt, the gods one day amused themselves by shooting and throwing at him, laughing gaily as the objects they threw fell short or turned aside. Now Loki, the God of Fire, was bitterly jealous of the God of Light, and, as he watched the sport, his evil nature prompted him to a cruel and cowardly deed. Having discovered that the mistletoe

alone of all created things had made no promise,
Loki hastened to the gate of Valhalla, where the
mistletoe was growing, and plucking it, by the
help of his magical power quickly fashioned
from it an arrow. He then returned and sought
out Hodur, who, because of his blindness, was
standing idly aside and taking no part in the
sport. Loki pretended to take pity on him, and
fitting the arrow to a bow which he placed in
Hodur's hands, he offered to aim the shaft for
the blind god. Aided by Loki, Hodur let fly
the fatal arrow, and, to the horror and amaze-
ment of the gods, Balder fell dead. The anger
of the gods against Hodur knew no bounds, and
they would have killed him had it not been
for their own law, which forbade the shedding
of blood in Asgard, the home of the gods. All
Asgard was plunged in the deepest grief, and
Hermod, the messenger of the gods, was sent to
Hel, the Goddess of the Underworld, praying
her to restore Balder to life. Hel consented to
do so, on condition that all created things should
weep for Balder. Messengers were at once sent
out over all the world to bid all things weep for
Balder. Living creatures, trees, and flowers,
and even the stones shed tears for the god they

had loved so well; but at last a giantess was found whose only reply to the messengers was " Let Hel keep what she has". Thus the evil Loki, for he it was in the disguise of a giantess, showed once again his cruel hatred of Balder, and caused the whole earth to mourn the loss of the radiant God of Light.

The gods now prepared for the burial of Balder. As was the custom among the Northmen, fuel was piled on the deck of Balder's ship *Ringhorn*, and the body was then laid on the funeral pyre. The sides of the ship were decorated with rich cloth and garlands of flowers, and swords, armour, drinking-vessels, and many other things which the gods valued, were placed beside the hero. A torch was then put to the fuel, and the ship was launched. The funeral pyre floated slowly towards the west, the rising flames lighting up sea and sky, until at last, like the sun itself, it sank slowly into the sea, and all light faded from the sky.

Balder's Funeral Pyre

But when the gods and heroes heard, they brought
The wood to Balder's ship, and built a pile,
Full the deck's breadth, and lofty; then the corpse
Of Balder on the highest top they laid.
And they set jars of wine and oil to lean
Against the bodies, and stuck torches near,
Splinters of pine-wood, soak'd with turpentine;
And brought his arms and gold, and all his stuff,
And slew the dogs who at his table fed,
And his horse—Balder's horse—whom most he loved,
And placed them on the pyre, and Odin threw
A last choice gift thereon, his golden ring.
The mast they fixt, and hoisted up the sails,
Then they put fire to the wood; and Thor
Set his stout shoulder hard against the stern
To push the ship through the thick sands;—sparks flew
From the deep trench she plough'd, so strong a god
Furrow'd it; and the water gurgled in.
And the ship floated on the waves, and rock'd.
But in the hills a strong east wind arose,
And came down moaning to the sea; first squalls
Ran black o'er the sea's face, then steady rush'd
The breeze, and fill'd the sails, and blew the fire.
And wreathed in smoke the ship stood out to sea.
Soon with a roaring rose the mighty fire,
And the pile crackled; and between the logs
Sharp, quivering tongues of flame shot out, and leapt,
Curling and darting, higher, until they lick'd
The summit of the pile, the dead, the mast,

The Day of the Sun

And ate the shrivelling sails; but still the ship
Drove on, ablaze above her hull with fire.
And the gods stood upon the beach, and gazed.
And while they gazed, the sun went lurid down
Into the smoke-wrapt sea, and night came on.
Then the wind fell with night, and there was calm;
But through the dark they watch'd the burning ship
Still carried o'er the distant waters on,
Farther and farther, like an eye of fire.
And long, in the far dark, blazed Balder's pile;
But fainter, as the stars rose high, it flared,
The bodies were consumed, ash choked the pile.
And as, in a decaying winter-fire,
A charr'd log, falling, makes a shower of sparks—
So with a shower of sparks the pile fell in,
Reddening the sea around; and all was dark.

MATTHEW ARNOLD—*Balder Dead.*

CHAPTER XV

Monday—The Day of the Moon

The moon, like the sun, was an object of wonder in the days of old, and was worshipped almost everywhere in some form or other, but it does not play quite so important a part in story as the sun. Since the moon is paler than the sun and its light soft and gentle, it was often regarded as being a chariot driven by a woman, but the course of the moon-goddess across the sky was similar to that of the sun-god.

Diana, the moon-goddess of the Greeks and Romans, known also as Cynthia, Phœbe, and Artemis, was the twin-sister of Apollo, and drove a golden chariot drawn by milk-white horses. Diana and Apollo were children of Jupiter, and were born in the Island of Delos, where a temple to Apollo was afterwards built. Another of the Seven Wonders of the World was the temple to Diana at Ephesus, on the west coast of Asia

Minor. The worship of Diana at Ephesus is mentioned in the Acts of the Apostles: "And when the town clerk had quieted the multitude, he saith, 'Ye men of Ephesus, what man is there who knoweth not how that the city of the Ephesians is temple-keeper of the great Diana and of the image which fell down from Jupiter?'" The temple was destroyed in the year A.D. 263, but remains of it may still be seen.

Diana was also the Goddess of Hunting; she was a skilled archer, and spent the day in hunting, as we have seen in the story of Orion.

The most famous story of Diana is that of her love for Endymion, a young shepherd—a story which has been told by the poets many times. One evening as the moon-goddess was driving silently across the sky, she saw sleeping on a hillside a handsome youth, his resting flock scattered over the gentle slope. Attracted by his beauty, Diana stepped from her chariot and gazed long at his face; then softly stooping, she kissed him lightly on the lips. Endymion, half wakened by her touch, caught a fleeting vision of the fair goddess as she hastened to her chariot. Filled with wonder at the sight, he rose quickly and rubbed his eyes, but all he saw was the bright moon floating across the dark sky, and he thought that he had been dreaming. The next night the goddess came to him again, and again he saw her with his half-closed eyes. Each night when the bright rays of the moon fell on his upturned face he dreamed this wonderful dream, but he was always sleeping when the goddess came, and never saw her in her full and dazzling beauty. The days now seemed long and dreary to Endymion, and he waited anxiously for the night that he might see again the glorious vision.

Diana was filled with dread at the thought that the beautiful youth would lose his beauty as the years went by, and at last she cast a spell over him while he slept, so that he should never wake again, and carried him away to a cave in a mountain-side known only to herself. There the loving Diana paused each night in her journey across the sky, and gazed on the face of the fair Endymion.

Diana, when hunting in the forest, was attended by a band of wood-nymphs who were her faithful followers. One of these nymphs, Arethusa, was one day cooling herself after the chase on the banks of the River Alpheus, when suddenly the God of the River appeared. The startled nymph ran quickly into the woods, but the god Alpheus pursued her, telling her that he loved her and that she need fear no harm. Arethusa was too frightened to listen to the god, and ran on, till at last, worn out, she prayed to Diana for help. The moon-goddess was ever ready to help her faithful nymphs, and in answer to the prayer transformed the girl into a fountain, which she hid in a thick mist. Alpheus, suddenly losing sight of the nymph, wandered sorrowfully about, calling out her name in his distress. Arethusa now thought that she was safe, but the wind-god, Zephyrus, blew aside the mist, and Alpheus saw a fountain where there had not been one before, and guessed what had happened. He quickly changed himself into a river and rushed towards the fountain, but Arethusa sprang from the rocks and hastened away over the stones and grass. Diana now saw her fresh danger, and made an opening in the ground, through which Arethusa slipped, to find herself in the kingdom of Pluto, the God of the Underworld. Here she wandered until she found another opening, by which she escaped once again into the sunshine on the plain of Sicily. Alpheus, however, at last made his way across the sea to Sicily, where he found Arethusa and won her love. The Greeks believed that flowers cast into the River Alpheus in Greece were carried by the river as gifts to his lover, and appeared later in the fountain of Arethusa in Sicily!

Among the Egyptians the moon was regarded as a god, who was named Thoth (The Measurer). He was also the God of Wisdom, Invention, Writing, and Magic. He was one of the earliest of the Egyptian gods, having come into being at the same time as Ra, the sun-god, and it was he who was said to have created the world. The Romans compared him with Mercury because, like Mercury, he invented writing. As the God of the Moon, he was represented as wearing a crescent moon on his head, and holding in his hand a stylus, a pointed instrument used by the Egyptians for writing on their wax tablets.

The Babylonian moon-god was Sin, the Lord of Wisdom. He was the father of the sun-god, and was one of the greatest of the gods, owing to the fact that the Babylonians regulated their calendar by the moon.

The Angles and Saxons believed that the moon was driven across the sky by Mani, the son of a giant, in a golden chariot drawn by a horse

named the All Swift. As in the case of the sun,
our ancestors had no distinct goddess of the
moon; but we shall read of Mani again in a
later chapter.

Hymn to Diana

Queen and huntress, chaste and fair,
　Now the sun is laid to sleep,
Seated in thy silver chair,
　　State in wonted manner keep:
　　　Hesperus entreats thy light,
　　　Goddess excellently bright.

Earth, let not thy envious shade
　Dare itself to interpose;
Cynthia's shining orb was made
　　Heaven to clear when day did close;
　　　Bless us then with wishèd sight,
　　　Goddess excellently bright.

Lay thy bow of pearl apart,
　And thy crystal shining quiver;
Give unto the flying hart
　　Space to breathe, how short soever,
　　　Thou that mak'st a day of night,
　　　Goddess excellently bright.

　　　　　BEN JONSON—*Cynthia's Revels.*

CHAPTER XVI

Tuesday—The Day of Tiu

Tuesday is the first day of the week which is named after a god of the Angles and Saxons— Tiu, the God of War. The Angles and Saxons, like the Greeks and Romans, worshipped many gods, and though these gods were in a great number of ways similar to those of the Greeks and Romans, we also find very great differences. These differences are due to the fact that the Angles and Saxons lived in a very different kind of country, led a very different kind of life, and consequently had different ideas. Their chief enemies were frost and cold, and they imagined the freezing winds to be caused by frost-giants who lived in a land of ice and waged continual warfare with the gods who befriended man and protected him as far as they could against the frost-giants and all the suffering which they caused. The chief of these gods was Woden or Odin, the All-father, of whom we read in the following chapter, and next to him in importance came Thor, the God of Thunder, the bitterest enemy of the giants. The god after whom Tuesday is named was known as Tiu among the Angles and Saxons, and as Tyr among the Norsemen. He was the God of War, and corresponds to Mars among the Romans, whose name for this day was *Dies Martis*, the day of Mars. The French have kept the Roman name in the form *mardi*.

Tiu was a great fighter and knew no fear, and was naturally always called upon in time of battle. He was usually represented as having no right hand, owing to a misfortune which befell him in the following way. From his lofty throne Odin, the chief of the gods, one day saw in the land of the giants three terrible monsters, which grew so rapidly that he was filled with fear lest they should invade the home of the gods. Accordingly he determined to get rid of them before they became any stronger. One Hel, an enormous giantess, he flung into the Underworld, where, as the Goddess of Death, she ruled over the kingdom of the dead. Another, Iormungandr, a serpent, he cast into the sea, where it grew so huge that it encircled the whole earth. The third was Fenrir, a wolf, whom Odin brought to Asgard, the home of the gods, hoping that he might eventually tame him. Fenrir, however, grew stronger and fiercer each day, until the gods, of whom Tiu alone was brave enough to go near him, decided at last to bind him in such a way that he could do no harm. A very strong chain was obtained, and the gods suggested to Fenrir, who often boasted of his great strength, that he should allow himself to be bound with it in order to prove whether he was really as strong as he claimed to be. Fenrir agreed, and then by merely stretching himself easily broke his bonds. Again the gods put him to the test with a still stronger chain, but as before he succeeded in breaking it. Seeing that no ordinary chain would be strong enough to bind Fenrir, the gods sent one of their servants to the home of the dwarfs, a race of little people who lived under-ground, and who were very clever workers in metal. They also possessed great powers of magic, as we shall see in a later story. At the bidding of the gods, the dwarfs made a silken rope out of the voice of fishes, a woman's beard, the roots of a mountain, and the footsteps of a cat, which was so strong that no power could

break it! A third time the gods challenged
Fenrir to show his strength by allowing himself
to be bound with this new cord, but Fenrir
became suspicious, and at last consented only
on condition that one of the gods should put his
hand in his mouth, and hold it there as a pledge
that the gods were not deceiving him. This
condition greatly alarmed the gods, who began
to fear that their trick was not going to succeed,
but the bold war-god Tiu stepped forward and,
without any hesitation, placed his right hand in
the wolf's mouth. The gods at once bound
Fenrir with the magic cord made by the dwarfs,
and, in spite of all his struggles, the wolf was
unable to free himself. Great was the delight of
the gods at their success, a delight shared by all
but Tiu, who had little cause to be pleased with
the result of the trick, for Fenrir, finding he
was trapped, immediately bit off the hand of the
god. Thus Tiu was deprived of his sword hand,
but so clever was he that he wielded his sword
equally well with his left hand, and still remained
invincible in battle.

On one occasion Tiu and Thor, the God of
Thunder, set out for the land of the giants to
obtain an enormous kettle, which the gods re-

quired for a feast. They came at last to the home of a giant, Hymir, who possessed a kettle a mile deep and a mile wide, and were hospitably received by the giant's wife. When she learned the errand on which they had come, she warned them that her husband was very fierce and hot-tempered, and advised them to hide themselves when Hymir returned, lest he should kill them with a glance. No sooner had the gods taken refuge behind some kettles, which were kept on a beam at the end of the hall, than Hymir came in. When he heard that visitors had called, he flashed his eyes round the hall so fiercely that, as his glance lighted on the gods' hiding-place, the beam split in two, the kettles came crashing to the ground, and Tiu and Thor were discovered. Hymir, however, was persuaded by his wife to receive the gods kindly; he prepared a meal of three oxen in their honour, but was astonished and dismayed to see Thor eat two of them him-self. The next day the gods gave the giant many proofs of their great strength and skill, and Hymir consented to give them the kettle they were seeking. Tiu at once tried to lift it but failed; then Thor, after a mighty struggle, raised it from the ground, and, as he gave the final pull,

ODIN

From the statue by B. E. Fogelberg

[*Page 108*

his feet broke through the floor of the giant's house. As soon as the gods had departed, Thor carrying the kettle on his head, Hymir called his brothers together, and pursued after them. Thor, however, attacked them with his famous hammer, and killed them one by one. Tiu and Thor then continued their journey, and brought the huge kettle safely to their own land.

There are few stories told of Tiu, yet he held a high place among the gods, as the name Tuesday shows. He is most famous for his share in the binding of Fenrir, whereby was put off the dreaded Ragnarok, the day of the final battle between the gods and the giants.

CHAPTER XVII

Wednesday—The Day of Woden

Woden, or Odin as the Norsemen called him, was the chief of the gods of our ancestors, and corresponds to the Jupiter of the Romans. Also, for reasons which we shall read later, he was similar to Mercury, and his name was given to the Roman *Dies Mercurii*, day of Mercury, which still survives in the French *mercredi*.

As in the case of Jupiter and the Titans, Odin led the Northern gods in a gigantic struggle with the giants of ice and frost, and finally overthrew them. With the help of the gods, he then fashioned the world from the body of the chief of the giants. From the flesh he made the earth, known as Midgard (middle garden), and from his blood the sea, while from his bones he made the mountains, from his teeth the cliffs, and from his hair the trees. The giant's skull was then fixed over the earth to form the vault of the sky, and was held in place at the four corners by four dwarfs, Nordri, Sudri, Austri, and Westri, from whom we have obtained the names North, South, East, and West. Next the gods made the sun and moon, which were placed in golden chariots driven by Sol and Mani, the daughter and son of a giant who had named his children after the newly-created sun and moon. The Northmen thought that they could see on the moon the outline of two children carrying a pail, and the story goes that Mani, while travelling across the sky, one night caught up two children, Hiuki and Bil, who were compelled by their cruel father to carry water all night. Hiuki and Bil are still known to us in the familiar story of Jack and Jill. The sun and moon were said to be pursued continually by two fierce wolves, whose shapes could be seen in the clouds, and who, if they caught them up, would swallow them and plunge the world in darkness. Sometimes they nearly succeeded, and thus caused the eclipses.

Having completed the earth and peopled it with men and women, the gods, led by Odin, built magnificent palaces for themselves in Asgard, their home. The most famous of these was Valhalla, to which the bravest and mightiest of the mortals who fell in battle were summoned at their death. The walls of Valhalla were made of spears, and golden shields formed the roof. In the hall stood long tables, at which the dead heroes feasted.

The Northmen honoured a great fighter above all men, and they even thought it a disgrace for him to die in any other way than sword in hand. The great ambition of every fighting man was to be called to Valhalla after his death, there to spend his time in fighting and feasting. The fortunate ones were chosen from among the slain on the battle-fields by the Valkyries, Odin's battle-maidens, whose horses carried them through the air and over the sea. They rode among the storm-clouds, and the flash of their spears was seen in the lightning.

Odin was often pictured as sitting on a throne from which he could see the whole world, and wearing a suit of armour, covered with a blue mantle, which represented the sky. In his hand he held a famous spear, Gungnir, which never missed its mark. On his shoulders sat two ravens, Thought and Memory, which he sent out into the world every day to obtain news of all that happened. Like Tiu, the God of War, Odin suffered from a disfigurement, having lost one of his eyes. This loss is explained in the following story.

After the creation of the world, Odin wished to obtain great wisdom which would place him far above the other gods. This he could only procure from Mimir's spring, in whose clear waters the future was mirrored. Odin, therefore, visited Mimir and begged a draught of the wonderful water, but Mimir would only grant the request in return for one of Odin's eyes. The god was willing to make even this sacrifice for the great knowledge the water would give him, and accordingly he plucked out one of his eyes and gave it to Mimir, who sank it deep in the spring where it could always be seen shining. Odin then drank deep of the water, and thus gained the wisdom for which he was always famous.

All the life of the world, including even the lives of the gods, was said to depend on an enormous ash tree, Yggdrasil, the Tree of Life. This tree was created by Odin, and had three roots, one in the Underworld, another in Midgard, near Mimir's spring, and the third in Asgard. It grew to such a height that it overtopped the

whole world, and in its topmost branches sat an
eagle with a falcon between its eyes. The falcon
could see all three kingdoms, and reported all
that happened in them to the gods. In the
Underworld was a dragon, which continually
gnawed the roots of Yggdrasil in order to destroy
it and so bring about the downfall of the gods.
To prevent this disaster, the tree was daily
watered from a fountain in Asgard, whose magic
waters kept it continually green.

Joining Asgard and the earth was a bridge
made of fire, earth, and water, whose colours
were those of the rainbow. This bridge was
guarded against the giants by a god named Heimdall, whose sight and hearing were so keen that
he could see a hundred leagues by night as well
as by day, and could hear the grass growing on
the earth and the wool on the sheep's back! He
was armed with a flashing sword, and carried
a horn with which he was to give warning when
the giants should come against Asgard.

Odin was the inventor of Runes, the first
alphabet of the Northmen. The letters consisted almost entirely of straight lines placed in
different groups and positions, and were thought
at first to have a magical meaning. Each god

had a special rune or sign, and the use of the sign was supposed to bring help from the god. Thus all fighters carved the rune of Tiu on their swords in order that they might have his aid in battle. Runes were afterwards used in the ordinary way for writing, and very old runes have been found carved on stones in Scandinavia and in England. As the inventor of runes, Odin is like Mercury, who was supposed to have given the Romans their alphabet.

In addition to being the wisest of the gods, the inventor of runes, and the God of Eloquence, Odin was also the God of Poetry. The gift of poetry was guarded very jealously by the gods, and was only granted to mortals in special cases. Odin obtained the gift for himself and the other gods only with great difficulty. Hidden away in a hollow mountain, and carefully watched over by a giantess, were three vessels containing a magic fluid, which gave to anyone who drank of it the gift of poetry and song. Odin, knowing of this magic drink, determined to obtain it. Accordingly he set out for the land of the giants, dressed as a mortal, and wearing a broad-brimmed hat to hide the fact that he had only one eye. He hired himself as a servant to Baugi, the brother of the giant Suttung, to whom the vessels belonged, and asked as payment for his labour one draught of the magic fluid. As soon as his work was finished, Odin demanded payment, but Baugi was afraid to ask his brother for the drink, and suggested they should win it for themselves by trickery. They came to the mountain where the vessels were hidden, and bored a hole right through to the cave inside. Odin then changed himself into a snake and wriggled through the hole, just in time to escape the giant, who tried to kill him as he entered the hole. Having found his way into the cave, Odin again took on the form of a god, and begged the giantess who watched over the vessels to allow him just a sip of the magic drink. The giantess at last consented, but Odin, instead of taking a sip, quickly emptied all the vessels, and then, making his way out of the cave, transformed himself into an eagle and flew swiftly towards Asgard. He soon discovered, however, that the giant Suttung was pursuing him, also in the form of an eagle. As he neared Asgard the gods caught sight of him, and, seeing that the giant was gaining on Odin, they gathered together a great quantity of fuel and piled it on the palace walls. Immediately Odin had passed over the wall the gods set fire to the fuel, and the flames rose so high that the wings of the pursuing giant were scorched, and he fell into the fire and was burnt.

Odin seldom used this precious gift of poetry himself, but imparted it to his son Bragi, who became the minstrel of the gods and sang many songs in honour of the gods and the great heroes in Valhalla. All the singers among men, the bards, or scalds, as they were sometimes called, were thought to have received the gift from Odin, and were greatly honoured for that reason.

The Creation of the World

In the beginning, ere the Gods were born,
Before the Heavens were builded, thou didst slay
The giant Ymir, whom the abyss brought forth,
Thou and thy brethren fierce, the sons of Bor,
And cast his trunk to choke the abysmal void.
But of his flesh and members thou didst build
The earth and ocean, and above them Heaven.
And from the flaming world, where Muspel reigns,
Thou sent'st and fetched'st fire, and madest lights,
Sun, moon, and stars, which thou hast hung in Heaven,
Dividing clear the paths of night and day.
And Asgard thou didst build, and Midgard fort.

MATTHEW ARNOLD—*Balder Dead*

The Heroes of Valhalla

And all the Gods, and all the Heroes, woke.
And from their beds the Heroes rose, and donn'd
Their arms, and led their horses from the stall,
And mounted them, and in Valhalla's court,
Were ranged; and then the daily fray began.
And all day long they there are hack'd and hewn,
'Mid dust, and groans, and limbs lopp'd off, and blood;
But all at night returned to Odin's hall,
Woundless and fresh; such lot is theirs in heaven.
And the Valkyries on their steeds went forth
Tow'rd earth and fights of men; and at their side
Skulda, the youngest of the Nornies, rode;
And over Bifrost, where is Heimdall's watch,
Past Midgard fortress, down to earth they came;
There through some battle-field, where men fall fast,
Their horses fetlock-deep in blood, they ride,
And pick the bravest warriors out for death,
Whom they bring back with them at night to heaven
To glad the Gods, and feast in Odin's hall.

MATTHEW ARNOLD—*Balder Dead.*

CHAPTER XVIII

Thursday—The Day of Thor

Thor, the Thunderer, is perhaps the most famous of the gods of the Northmen, and was considered by some to be greater even than Odin. He was the God of the Peasants—the poor people, while Odin was thought more of by the rich people and the great fighters. Thor usually rode in a chariot of brass, drawn by two goats, Tooth-cracker and Tooth-gnasher, and it was this chariot which was supposed to make the thunder; hence Thor's name. Thor, alone of all the gods, was never allowed to cross the bridge joining Asgard and the earth, lest this chariot should break it down.

As the Thunderer, Thor corresponded to Jupiter, who, as we have read, hurled thunderbolts when enraged, and for this reason Thor's name was given to the Roman *Dies Jovis*, the day of Jupiter, the modern French *jeudi*.

Thor was of very great strength, like Hercules among the Greeks and Romans, and possessed a wonderful hammer called Miolnir, the Crusher, which always returned to his hand when he had thrown it at an enemy. He also wore a magic belt which increased his strength the more he pulled it in. The way in which Miolnir came to be made is told in a story of Thor's wife Sif, who was very proud of her golden hair, which reached down to her feet. One morning Thor woke to find that Sif's hair had been cruelly cut off during the night. Filled with anger, he set out to find the culprit, whom he rightly guessed to be Loki, the God of Fire. Loki was the spirit of evil and mischief, and was always playing cruel tricks on the gods, who frequently punished him. Thor soon caught Loki, and would have strangled him had he not promised to bring Sif a new head of hair as beautiful as the first. Thor then released Loki, who quickly went to the home of the dwarfs, who lived underground. There he found a dwarf who agreed to make the hair for Loki, and also presents for Odin and Frey, the God of the Fields, whom Loki was afraid would be angry with him. The dwarf made a head of hair of the finest gold thread, which he said would grow on

Sif's head as soon as it touched it. Then he made the spear Gungnir which, as we have seen, Odin always carried with him; while for Frey he made a ship which could sail through the air as well as on the water, and could be folded up like a cloth. Loki was of course delighted with the skill of this clever little smith, and declared that no other dwarf could be as clever. This led to a challenge from another dwarf, who claimed that he could make three still more wonderful things. This dwarf in his turn made a wild boar with golden bristles, which travelled through the air, and gave out a bright light as it passed; a magic ring, out of which came eight more rings exactly like it every ninth night; and lastly an iron hammer, Miolnir, which no one could resist. Loki and the dwarf then gave their presents to the gods: the spear and the ring to Odin, the ship and the golden boar to Frey, and the hair and the hammer to Thor. The gods decided that the contest had been won by the second dwarf, because Miolnir would be of such great use against the frost-giants, with whom the gods were continually fighting.

Thor often journeyed to the land of the giants, and on one occasion, having set out with Loki, he reached the desolate giant-country at night-fall. A thick mist covered the ground, and, after struggling on with some difficulty, the gods came to what seemed to be a house with an open door-way which took up all one side of the building. The gods entered the house, which was cold and dark, and, tired with their journey, lay down to sleep. Their rest, however, was soon disturbed by a loud noise and the trembling of the ground, and, fearing the roof of the house might fall on them, Thor and his companion moved into a smaller room which led out of the main building, and there slept till dawn. On going out into the open the next morning, Thor saw lying near an enormous giant, whose snores shook the ground, and was thus able to account for the noise and the trembling of the earth which had disturbed his sleep. But imagine the astonishment of the gods when the giant woke and picked up the house they had slept in—they had passed the night in the thumb of his glove! Thor and his companion then continued their journey, accompanied now by the giant, whose name was Skrymir. When evening came, they rested be-neath a tree, and the giant, before going to sleep, offered them the food which he carried in his

wallet. Thor, however, was unable to undo the
straps of the huge wallet, so the gods had to go
hungry. Angry at this, Thor dealt the giant,
who was now asleep, three terrible blows on the
head with his hammer Miolnir. But the only
effect this had on the giant was to cause him to
wake up and complain that three times a leaf or
a twig had fallen on his head. The next morning
Skrymir showed the gods the way to the castle of
Utgard-loki, the giant king, and then left them.
Arriving at the palace, the gods entered and pre-
sented themselves to the king, who recognized
them and asked them to show him their powers
of which he had heard so much. Loki, who was
very hungry, offered to eat more than anyone,
and the king's cook was matched against him.
They each stood at the end of a wooden trough
full of meat, and though Loki soon reached the
middle of the trough, leaving nothing but bones
behind, he found that the giant had eaten the
bones and the trough as well. Loki's defeat
made Thor even more anxious to show his
powers, and he offered to empty the largest
drinking-horn in the palace. A huge drinking-
horn was at once brought in, and Thor drank so
deep and so long that it seemed as if he would

never stop, only to find, however, when he could drink no more, that the horn was still almost full. Nothing daunted by his failure, Thor now offered to show his strength, but when he tried to lift Utgard-loki's cat, he only succeeded in raising one paw from the ground. Thor tried yet again to show his skill, this time in wrestling, but he was easily beaten by Utgard-loki's old nurse. The gods were then entertained by the giants till the following day, when they returned. Before they left, however, Utgard-loki explained that he was the giant Skrymir, and that he had used magic against the gods in all their contests. By magic he had placed a mountain between his head and Thor's hammer and thus saved his life, for the blows had made three huge clefts in the mountain. The cook who had beaten Loki was really Wild Fire; the end of the drinking-horn which Thor had failed to empty had been placed in the sea, which had sunk lower after Thor's enormous draughts; the cat was really the huge snake Iormungandr, which encircled the earth, and which Thor had nearly lifted out of the sea; the nurse was really Old Age, whom, of course, no one could possibly overcome.

Thor seldom lost an opportunity of making

THOR AND THE GIANTS

From the painting by M. E. Winge

[Page 123

war on the giants, and on a famous occasion
challenged to single combat the giant Hrungnir,
whose head and heart were of stone. Hrungnir
one day matched his horse Golden Mane against
Odin's steed, Sleipnir, and, in the excitement of
the race, followed Odin right to the gates of
Valhalla. Though, of course, the presence of
a giant in Asgard could not be allowed, the gods
had no wish to take advantage of Hrungnir's
mistake, and offered him meat and drink in their
banqueting hall. Hrungnir, however, drank too
freely of the mead of the gods, and began to
speak proud words and boast one day that he
would overthrow Asgard and kill all the gods.
This so enraged Thor that he raised his hammer
to kill Hrungnir, but the gods would not allow
him to shed blood within their home. He then
challenged the giant to a duel, which was arranged to take place three days later on the
boundary of Hrungnir's kingdom. At the appointed time the giant was on the chosen spot
awaiting his enemy, and, feeling the earth shaking beneath him, he stood on his shield of stone,
lest Thor should come up from the ground. But
no sooner had he done this than Thor suddenly
came in sight and hurled his hammer straight at

the giant's head. Hrungnir, having no shield, tried to ward off the hammer with his stone club, which was shattered to pieces, thus scattering flint stones over the whole earth, where they may still be found. One piece entered Thor's forehead, and he dropped fainting to the ground, but as he fell his hammer struck Hrungnir on the head and killed him. Thor was pinned to the ground by one of the giant's legs, and, after each of the gods had tried in vain to free him, he was at last rescued by Magni, his little son of three, who easily raised the giant's leg and released his father, receiving as a reward Hrungnir's horse, Golden Mane. Magni was one of the few gods destined to survive the terrible Ragnarok, the day of destruction, when, as we shall see, Thor, the Thunderer, fell in mortal combat with the sea-monster Iormungandr.

The Challenge of Thor

I am the God Thor,
I am the War God,
I am the Thunderer!
Here in my Northland,
My fastness and fortress,
Reign I for ever!

The Day of Thor

Here amid ice-bergs
Rule I the nations;
This is my hammer,
Miolner the mighty;
Giants and sorcerers
Cannot withstand it!

These are the gauntlets
Wherewith I wield it,
And hurl it afar off;
This is my girdle;
Whenever I brace it,
Strength is redoubled!

The light thou beholdest
Stream through the heavens,
In flashes of crimson,
Is but my red beard
Blown by the night-wind,
Affrighting the nations.

Jove is my brother;
Mine eyes are the lightning;
The wheels of my chariot
Roll in the thunder,
The blows of my hammer
Ring in the earthquake!

Force rules the world still,
Has ruled it, shall rule it;

Thursday

Meekness is weakness,
Strength is triumphant,
Over the whole earth,
Still is it Thor's-day!

LONGFELLOW—*The Saga of King Olaf.*

CHAPTER XIX

Friday—The Day of Freya

In the stories of the gods and goddesses of the Angles and Saxons we find two goddesses, Frigga, the wife of Odin and queen of the gods, and Freya, the Goddess of Love. Some people think that Friday was named after Frigga, and others that it was Freya's day. Since very similar stories are told of each of them, it is quite probable that they were really the same person. The Roman name for the day was *Dies Veneris*, the day of Venus, who, it will be remembered, was the Goddess of Love, and so corresponded to Freya. The modern French name is taken from the Latin and is *vendredi*.

Frigga was the Goddess of the Clouds, and, when she was not with her husband Odin, spent her time in spinning clouds. Her spinning-wheel was studded with jewels, and at night could be seen in the sky as the constellation

to which the Romans gave the name of Orion's
Belt, as we have seen in the story of Orion.

Frigga was also the Goddess of Spring, and
as such was known as Eastre, whom we have
already mentioned as giving us the word Easter.

Freya, the Goddess of Love and Beauty, like
the Venus of the Romans, received a great wel-
come when she came to the home of the gods,
and was given a special kingdom called Folk
Meadow, where was a vast hall known as the
Hall of Many Seats. Here she received half of
those slain in battle, the other half being entertained by Odin, as we have seen.

Freya is depicted as having blue eyes and
golden hair, and often as wearing a robe of
feathers, which enabled her to fly through the
air like a bird.

The goddess is said to have married Odur,
who was probably Odin under another name.
Odur once had occasion to leave Freya and
travel over the world, and the goddess was
broken-hearted at his departure. Her tears fell
among the rocks and were changed to gold,
while some which fell into the sea were transformed into amber. All nature mourned with
her: the trees shed their leaves, the grass

withered, and the flowers drooped their heads.
At last Freya in her distress set out to find her
husband, and, passing through many lands, where
her golden tears were afterwards found, came to
the sunny south, and there overtook the wandering Odur. As the lovers returned, the fields and
the flowers rejoiced with them. The frost and
snow fled before them, and the earth became
green again as they passed.

> " And Freya next came nigh, with golden tears;
> The loveliest Goddess she in Heaven, by all
> Most honour'd after Frea, Odin's wife.
> Her long ago the wandering Odur took
> To mate, but left her to roam distant lands;
> Since then she seeks him, and weeps tears of gold."
>
> MATTHEW ARNOLD—*Balder Dead.*

This story, of course, reminds us of Ceres and
Persephone, and is only another fanciful explanation of summer and winter.

Freya was the proud possessor of a dazzling
necklace of gold, which had been made by the
dwarfs, and which she wore night and day. On
one occasion only did she lend the necklace,
when Thor, disguised as Freya, went to the land
of the giants to recover his hammer, which had
been stolen by the giant Thrym. Loki, by bor-

rowing Freya's robe of feathers and flying over
the country of the giants, had discovered the
thief, but had also found that Thrym would only
return the hammer on condition that Freya
would become his wife. When Freya heard of
the giant's presumption, she became greatly enraged, and vowed that she would never leave her
beloved Odur and go to live in that dreary and
desolate land of cold. Heimdall, the guardian
of the bridge Bifrost, then suggested that Thor
should go to Thrym disguised as Freya, in company with Loki disguised as Freya's attendant.
The gods at last allowed themselves to be persuaded, and Thor, having borrowed Freya's
clothes and necklace and wearing a thick veil,
set out with Loki, who was dressed as a hand-
maiden. On reaching the giant's palace, they
were welcomed by Thrym, who was delighted at
the success of his plan, and who led them to the
banqueting hall, where a great feast was held.
At the end of the feast, Thrym ordered the
famous hammer to be brought in, and he himself
laid it in his bride's lap as a marriage gift.
Thor's hand immediately closed over the hammer,
and in a few moments Thrym and all the guests
invited to the wedding feast lay dead.

Freya was greatly relieved to have her necklace returned in safety, but the evil Loki, attracted by its wonderful beauty, determined to steal it. One night the god, by changing himself into a fly, succeeded in entering Freya's palace. He then resumed his own shape, and, creeping stealthily to Freya's bed, gently removed the necklace from the goddess's neck. The watchful Heimdall, however, had heard Loki's footsteps, and, looking in the direction of the Folk Meadow, became a witness of the theft. He at once set off in pursuit of Loki, and, overtaking him, drew his sword and was about to kill the thief, when Loki changed himself into a flame. Heimdall immediately changed himself into a cloud, and sent down a shower of rain to put out the fire. Loki then took the form of a bear, and opened his mouth to catch the water. Heimdall also took the form of a bear and attacked Loki, who, finding that he was being overpowered, changed himself yet again, into a seal. Heimdall followed suit, and fought again with Loki, and at length compelled him to give up the necklace, which was returned to Freya.

On another occasion Freya was sought by one of the giants, and it was only by the cunning of

Loki and by an act of bad faith on the part of
the gods that she was saved. The gods, ever
anxious lest the giants should invade Asgard,
decided to build a stronghold which would prove
impregnable. They received an offer from a
stranger, who was willing to undertake the work
in return for the sun, the moon, and the goddess Freya. By Loki's advice they accepted the
offer on condition that he should complete the
work in one winter, aided only by his horse.
To the surprise of the gods the stranger agreed
to these conditions, and with the help of his
horse, which could haul the heaviest stone, set
to work. The gods, who at first felt sure that
their conditions had made the task impossible,
were alarmed to find as time went on that the
stranger was working so quickly that it seemed
certain that he would be able to keep his promise. The gods on their side had no intention
whatever of keeping their promise, since they
could not possibly part with the sun and the
moon and the Goddess of Love, and they angrily
pointed out to Loki that since it was he who had
got them into this difficulty, he must find some
way out of it. Loki replied that the gods need
have no fear, for with his usual cunning he had

thought of a plan whereby the stranger might be made to forfeit his reward. On the last day, when only one stone remained to be dragged into position, Loki changed himself into a horse, and, trotting out from the forest, neighed loudly to attract the attention of the stranger's horse. Tired of his continual labour and longing for freedom and rest, the horse broke free from its load and galloped after Loki. The stranger, after pursuing it vainly through the forest, at last made his way to Asgard, and, full of anger at the trick which had been played upon him, took on his real shape, for he was a frost-giant, and was about to attack the gods when Thor hurled his hammer at him and killed him.

Frey, the god mentioned in the story of Loki and Sif's golden hair, was Freya's brother. He was the God of the Fields, and sacrifices were made to him for the crops. In the early spring his wooden image was driven in a chariot through the countryside, in order that he might bless the fields and bring a fruitful harvest. Frey, as we have seen, became the possessor of a ship which could travel over land and sea, and though large enough to contain all the gods, yet could be folded up like a cloth, and he also possessed a

boar with golden bristles. The god often rode
on this boar, which was swifter than a horse, and
was no doubt a symbol of the sun, which ripened
the crops. We find the same idea of sunshine
in Frey's flashing sword, which fought of its own
accord as soon as it was drawn from its sheath.

The month of the Angles and Saxons which
begins just before our Christmas was sacred to
both Frey and Thor, and it was customary at
that time, as we have already mentioned, to bind
a huge wooden wheel with straw, and, setting
fire to it, to roll it down a hill. The wheel was a
symbol of the sun, which at that time began to
chase away the winter. At this time, too, was
held a great feast to all the gods, and the chief
meat eaten was a boar's head, in honour of Frey.
The missionaries who first brought Christianity
to the Northmen, finding this feast was of great
importance and was celebrated by all the people,
did not try to do away with it. Instead, they
changed it from a heathen to a Christian festival
by putting Christ in the place of the Norse gods,
and calling it the Feast or Mass of Christ. A
similar change was made, it will be remembered,
in the case of the Easter festival, held in honour
of Eastre or Frigga, the wife of Odin.

he also played dangerous tricks on them, and more than once led them into harm. As time went on, he seems to have become the spirit of evil only, and the gods at last banished him from Asgard, and condemned him to a terrible punishment. He was chained to the side of a cave, and a snake was fastened over his head in such a way that the poison from its fangs dropped on his face. His wife, however, remained faithful to him; she made her way to the cave where Loki was imprisoned, and stayed by his side, holding up a cup to catch the poison which fell from the snake, and only leaving him in order to empty the cup when it was full. The poison which fell on Loki's face while she was absent caused him to twist and writhe with pain till he shook the earth, and thus produced earthquakes.

This punishment of Loki reminds us of the story of Prometheus, but it will be remembered that the latter suffered because he had been a friend to man, and not like Loki a source of evil. As Prometheus was rescued at last by Hercules, so Loki was destined to escape on the great day of Ragnarok, and to appear in his true colours on the side of the giants, soon afterwards meeting his death at the hands of Heimdall. The

Northmen, unlike the Greeks and Romans, regarded their gods as mortal, and believed that
their rule would one day come to an end. They
pictured a final struggle between the gods, the
forces of good, and the forces of evil represented
by Loki, the frost-giants, and all the terrible
monsters which they had created. Odin, in his
great wisdom, knew what the future would
eventually bring, and spared no effort to prolong
his rule and prepare for the fateful day. For
this reason he welcomed the great heroes to
Valhalla, and kept the tree of life, Yggdrasil,
nourished with the water of the sacred spring;
for this reason the giants tried to steal Thor's
hammer, the weapon they most dreaded. Many
things pointed to the approach of Ragnarok.
First the earth suffered from six successive
winters more severe and prolonged than had
ever been known before. Snow fell without
ceasing, freezing winds blew from the north, and
the whole earth was covered with ice. In their
struggle to live under these terrible conditions,
men lost their faith in the gods, and gave themselves up to evil and wrong-doing. Sin and
crime were found everywhere, and as the evil-
doers passed into the Underworld, they became

food for the wolves which were continually pursuing the sun and moon, and endeavouring to swallow them. As their food became more plentiful, the wolves increased in strength and speed, until at last the day came when Sol and Mani found the wolves rapidly gaining on them. In spite of all their efforts, the wolves continued to overtake them, and at length seized them in their enormous jaws, and plunged the earth into darkness. The foundations of the earth shook, the stars fell from the sky, and the mountains came crashing down. As if this were a signal, Loki and the fierce wolf Fenrir put forth new strength and burst their chains, for their day of revenge had come. The dragon which lay at the foot of Yggdrasil gnawed through the root of the sacred tree. The Midgard serpent, Iormungandr, lashed and writhed till the sea rose in mighty waves, and at last breaking its bonds, the terrible monster crawled to the land. Heimdall, the keeper of the bridge, realizing that the twilight of the gods was at hand, blew a blast on his horn that was heard in every corner of the world. The gods hastily donned their armour, and marshalled the army of heroes. Now indeed Odin regretted the loss of his eye,

Tiu that he had sacrificed his right hand, and Frey that he had lent his sword to his servant, who was away in the lands of the North.

Meanwhile the followers of the goddess Hel were led by Loki to the plain of Vigrid, the scene of the great battle. Here they were joined by Hel herself, Garm, the fierce dog who guarded the entrance to the Underworld, and Fenrir, the monster wolf. From the misty land of the North came the army of the frost-giants, while out of the South, with a burst of light, there dashed on to the plain Surtr, the giant of the Flaming Sword.

Terrible indeed were the forces arrayed against the gods, but they, like the Northmen themselves, knew no fear on the day of battle, and assembled their armies on the plain of Vigrid, prepared to resist the powers of evil to the last.

With shouts and cries, amid fire and smoke, the armies meet. Odin and the wolf Fenrir come together with a crash, which echoes through the whole world, but not even the mighty Odin can withstand this terrible enemy. Fenrir, now fiercer and stronger than ever before, opens his vast jaws till they stretch from heaven to earth, and overwhelms the leader of gods and men. But

Odin's death is quickly avenged. His son Vidar, wearing the iron shoe, which had been kept for this day, now falls upon Fenrir, and, as had been foretold, places his iron-shod foot on the monster's lower jaw, and then seizing the upper jaw, with a mighty wrench tears Fenrir asunder.

Meanwhile Tiu grapples with Garm, and after a fierce struggle slays him, only to fall dead beside him. Frey attacks the fire-giant Surtr, but soon falls before his flaming onslaught. Heimdall and Loki once again meet in deadly conflict, and this time Heimdall overcomes the God of Evil, but, like Tiu, falls mortally wounded by his enemy. Thor, with his hammer Miolnir, advances against the huge Midgard serpent. The struggle is long and terrible; with a mighty blow of his hammer Thor at last kills the monster, and then, as he staggers back, is overwhelmed by the flood of poison which it outpours. The heroes of Valhalla are all overthrown by the giants and the followers of Hel, and there is no longer anyone of Odin's vast host to withstand the powers of evil.

Surtr then flings his fire over the world, Asgard is consumed in roaring flames, and the earth, scorched and blackened, sinks into a boiling sea.

Ragnarok has come, and the old gods have passed away.

But in the minds of the Northmen evil could have no lasting victory. The very flames which had destroyed the home of the gods and had overwhelmed the earth had purged the world of evil. A new earth rose from the sea, lit by a new sun, the daughter of Sol, and life, drawn forth by its warm rays, once more spread over the earth. Trees clothed themselves anew with leaves, and the fields became fair with flowers. From the depth of the forest, where Mimir's spring had bubbled forth, came Lifthrasir (Desire of Life) and his wife Lif (Life), who in course of time became the rulers of a new race. To the field of Ida, where the gods had been wont to hold their games, came the survivors of the gods: two sons of Odin, Vidar, the slayer of Fenrir, and his brother Vali, who had killed Hodur to avenge the death of Balder; two sons of Thor, Magni (Strength) and Modi (Courage), who had rescued Miolnir from the battle-field and now wielded it in place of their father; and finally, Balder and Hodur, who had been set free from Hel, and who now lived together as brothers, forgetful of the past.

It seems strange to us that the Northmen should have pictured the destruction of their gods, and it is possible that the writers of the wonderful poems from which we obtain these stories knew something of Christianity, and had begun to turn from their heathen beliefs. We find, however, that many heathen peoples had similar beliefs. The idea of eternity was impossible to them; they felt that there must be an end to everything. Accordingly they imagined their gods, after a long period of peace and good rule, being overthrown by the powers of evil and destruction, and being replaced by a new heaven and earth, which in turn would also be destroyed and renewed. Among no other people do we find so complete a description of this world catastrophe as in our ancestors' story of Ragnarok, the Twilight of the Gods.

The Day of Ragnarok

The generations pass, the ages grow,
And bring us nearer to the final day
When from the south shall march the fiery band,
And cross the bridge of heaven, with Lok for guide,
And Fenrir at his heel with broken chain;
While from the east the giant Rymer steers

His ship, and the great serpent makes to land;
And all are marshall'd in one flaming square
Against the Gods, upon the plains of Heaven.

.   .   .   .

Far to the south, beyond the blue, there spreads
Another Heaven, the boundless—no one yet
Hath reach'd it; there hereafter shall arise
The second Asgard, with another name.
Thither, when o'er this present earth and Heavens
The tempest of the latter days hath swept,
And they from sight have disappear'd, and sunk,
Shall a small remnant of the Gods repair;
There re-assembling we shall see emerge
From the bright Ocean at our feet an earth
More fresh, more verdant than the last, with fruits
Self-springing, and a seed of man preserved,
Who then shall live in peace, as now in war.
But we in Heaven shall find again with joy
The ruin'd palaces of Odin, seats
Familiar, halls where we have supp'd of old;
Re-enter them with wonder, never fill
Our eyes with gazing, and rebuild with tears.
And we shall tread once more the well-known plain
Of Ida, and among the grass shall find
The golden dice wherewith we played of yore;
And that will bring to mind the former life
And pastime of the Gods, the wise discourse
Of Odin, the delights of other days.

MATTHEW ARNOLD—*Balder Dead.*

CHAPTER XXI

The Meaning of the Ancient Myths

It is perhaps difficult for us to realize that the wonderful gods and goddesses of whom we have been reading were once very real to the people who invented them, but the fact that they are commemorated for all time in the names of our months and days shows how real they were. Some of the stories may seem childish to us, and the ideas which they contain are certainly very different from the ideas of God we have to-day. But it must always be remembered that very nearly all that we know about the marvellous world in which we live has been discovered since the days of the Romans and Northmen. They did not have the opportunity of learning what we have learnt, and if their belief seems childish to us, it is because in some ways the people were childish, when we compare them with ourselves. Grown-up people, however, do not make fun of the wonderful stories which children invent, and many of the myths, as these stories of the gods are called, are very clever and very beautiful.

The earth and the sea, the sun and the moon and the stars, the seasons, the rain and the snow, the trees and the flowers were all difficult to understand, and those early peoples explained them as best they could. Most of these explanations seem fanciful to us now, but, after all, they were very natural explanations. We shall see this better if we compare the gods and goddesses of the Greeks and Romans with those of the Northmen. They are very similar in many ways, and many of the stories are similar too.

Jupiter, before he became the ruler of the gods, had to overthrow the Titans, and in the same way Odin had to conquer the frost-giants. The Roman gods had their home on Mount Olympus, from which Jupiter could look down over the earth, while Odin from his palace in Asgard could also see all heaven and earth. Hel, the Goddess of the Underworld, reigned over a dark kingdom, to which came those who died, in the same way as Pluto ruled the underground kingdom of Hades. The Underworlds, too, were very similar; the good among the dead were divided off from the evil, who suffered terrible punishments for their crimes; the entrance in each case was guarded by a fierce dog, Garm in the kingdom of Hel, and the three-headed Cerberus in Hades.

We have already noticed the way in which the Romans and the Northmen explained summer and winter, and the likeness between the punishments of Prometheus and Loki.

In the sun-myths there is much confusion, for although the Greeks and the Romans had a sun-god, Apollo, and the Northmen a god of light, Balder the Beautiful, we find in some stories that the sun is represented by other gods, and even mortals. Frey is really the sun, for it is he who makes the crops grow in the fields, and light like the sun's rays flashes from his sword and from his golden-bristled boar. Juno is the light of heaven, and in the story of Argus, the Hundred-eyed, gives Io, who represents the moon, into the keeping of Argus, the starry sky, but the light of the stars is slowly put out by Mercury, the God of Wind and Rain. The burning of the earth by Phaeton means a drought which is brought to an end by a thunder-storm, the thunderbolt hurled at Phaeton by Jupiter.

In the story of Diana and Endymion, Endymion

is a symbol of the setting sun which Diana watches as she mounts the sky. Hercules, too, probably represents the sun. His conquest of the many-headed serpent is the victory of the sun over the darkness, as is Apollo's slaying of Python. The twelve labours of Hercules may represent the twelve constellations in the zodiac, or possibly twelve hours of daylight. Hercules' funeral pyre, which reddens the whole sky like the setting sun, is seen again in the burning of Balder and his ship *Ringhorn*.

Thor is like Hercules, through his great strength, and just as he put on a woman's dress in order to recover his hammer from the giants, so Hercules on one occasion was forced to dress like a woman. Thor's wife, Sif, represents the earth, while her golden hair is the vegetation. When Loki steals the hair, he brings the same misfortune on the earth as Pluto causes by seizing Persephone. Loki has to visit the dwarfs underground in order to obtain the golden hair, and Mercury seeks Persephone in Hades. Persephone's eating of the pomegranate seeds, which keeps her in the Underworld, is like the refusal of the giantess to weep for Balder.

Another sun-myth is the story of Jason, who

obtains the Golden Fleece (the rays of the sun) by killing the dragon, which represents either darkness or drought. Phryxus and Helle represent clouds, as probably do the Argo and the magic ship of Frey. Bellerophon, too, is the sun, who, mounted on Pegasus, the clouds, slays the dragon of drought, and at last, when struck by Jupiter's thunderbolt, falls from the sky into darkness.

We see then that all these myths were attempts to explain or describe what we call Nature—the earth and the sky, the sun, the moon, and so on. As Christianity spread, belief in the myths passed away, but many interesting and curious stories have been left behind which cannot be forgotten as long as we keep the names of our months and days. These names will always remind us of gods and heroes, of stirring deeds and bold adventures, all of which have been preserved too in the writings of the great poets of all times and lands.

CHAPTER XXII

Notes on Certain Days

Sabbath Day.—The word *sabbath* comes from a Hebrew word meaning "to cease from labour", and the Sabbath Day, as we know from the Bible, was the seventh day of the week and a day of rest. It is owing to this custom of the Jews that our Sunday is a holiday. The word "holiday" means, of course, "holy day", and we owe all our holidays in the first place to the custom of keeping certain Saint's Days as days of rest from work, in order that festivities might be held in honour of the saint of the day.

Black Monday.—This name is given nowadays to any Monday on which a great disaster happens, but it originated in 1360, when a terrible storm did great damage in England on the Easter Monday of that year. Shakespeare refers to this Black Monday in his play *The Merchant of Venice*, Act II, Scene 5.

Shrove Tuesday.—The day before Ash Wednesday, and so named because on that day people were expected to "shrive", that is, confess their sins to the priest. After the confession was over, the people made merry, and the pancakes connected with Shrove Tuesday are all that is left to us of the old feasting and merry-making.

Ash Wednesday.—The time from this day to Easter Day (forty days) is called "Lent" (from Old-English *lencten*: Spring, the time when the days grow *longer*), and it was once a general custom among Christians to fast during this period. Ash Wednesday is so called from a service of the Roman Catholic Church which is held on that day, and in the course of which the priests place ashes of burnt palm on the foreheads of penitents.

Maundy Thursday. — The Thursday before Good Friday. On this day was held the ceremony of washing the feet of poor people in memory of Christ's washing of His disciples' feet. This ceremony was called "Maundy", so the day became known as Maundy Thursday. Maundy comes from the Latin word *mandatum*, the first word of the service sung during the ceremony. Gifts were also made to the poor at the same

time, and this custom still continues. Every
Maundy Thursday money known as "Maundy
money" is given to a certain number of poor
people, the distribution of the money taking
place in Westminster Abbey. This money in-
cludes the old fourpenny - piece and twopenny
and one penny pieces in silver.

Lady Day.—The 25th of March, and the day
dedicated by the Church to the Virgin Mary
(Our Lady). The first of the four Quarter
Days.

Martinmas.—The 11th of November, the day
held by Roman Catholics as sacred to St.
Martin, Bishop of Tours, a town in France. He
served in the army for a number of years before
entering the Church, and many interesting tales
are told of him. He was born in A.D. 316, and
died in 400. Martinmas is the fourth of the
Scotch Quarter Days, the others being Candlemas,
Whitsunday, and Lammas.

Michaelmas Day.—The 29th of September, the
day on which the Mass or Feast of St. Michael
is held. St. Michael is described in the Book of
Daniel as being one of the chief of the angels.
Michaelmas is the third Quarter Day, the second
and fourth being Midsummer and Christmas.

Primrose Day.—The 19th of April, the day on which Benjamin Disraeli, Earl of Beaconsfield, died.   He was one of the Prime Ministers of Queen Victoria's reign.   The primrose was reputed to be his favourite flower, and his statue in Parliament Square is decorated with primroses each year on the anniversary of his death.

St. Swithin's Day.—St. Swithin lived in the reign of King Egbert.   He was the Bishop of Winchester, and died in A.D. 852.   He was buried outside the church at Winchester, and in 971, when the new cathedral had been built, the monks decided to place his body inside the cathedral.   They were prevented from doing so, however, by rain, which fell without ceasing for forty days.   This gave rise to the common belief that if it rains on St. Swithin's Day (15th July) it will rain for forty days.

St. Valentine's Day. — St. Valentine was a Christian bishop who was beheaded in Rome about the year A.D. 270.   His martyrdom is commemorated on the 14th. of February.   The custom of sending " valentines " on that day has really no connection with St. Valentine, but is probably an ancient Roman custom arising out of the worship of Juno.

Greek, Roman, and Old-English Gods

GREEK.	ROMAN.	OLD-ENGLISH.
Zeus.	Jupiter (King).	Woden.
Hera.	Juno (Queen).	Frigga.
Aphrodite.	Venus (Love).	Freya.
Ares.	Mars (War).	Tiu.
Hermes.	Mercury (Messenger).	Hermod.
Helios.	Apollo (Sun).	Frey, Balder.
Artemis.	Diana (Moon).	—
Athene.	Minerva (Wisdom).	—
Hephæstus.	Vulcan (Fire).	—
Poseidon.	Neptune (Sea).	—
Dionysius.	Bacchus (Wine).	—
—	—	Thor.
—	—	Loki.

Names of the Days

ROMAN.	OLD-ENGLISH.	FRENCH.
Dies Solis.	Sunnan-dæg.	Dimanche.
Dies Lunæ.	Monan-dæg.	Lundi.
Dies Martis.	Tiwes-dæg.	Mardi.
Dies Mercurii.	Wodnes-dæg.	Mercredi.
Dies Jovis.	Thures-dæg.	Jeudi.
Dies Veneris.	Frige-dæg.	Vendredi.
Dies Saturni.	Sæter-dæg.	Samedi.

The French Revolutionary Calendar

Vendémiaire (Wine).	Nivôse (Snowy).	Germinal (Budding).	Messidor (Harvest)
Brumaire (Foggy).	Pluviôse (Rainy).	Floréal (Flowery).	Thermidor (Hot).
Frimaire (Frosty).	Ventôse (Windy).	Prairial (Meadow).	Fructidor (Fruit).

Each month consisted of thirty days, and five extra days, dedicated to Virtue, Genius, Labour, Opinion, and Rewards, were put in as holidays to make up three hundred and sixty-five days. Every fourth year an extra day was added, known as Revolution Day. The Calendar dated from 22nd September, 1792, and was in force till the year 1806.